# World War Two: Time Chart

| YEAR | WAR IN WESTERN EUROPE | WAR IN EASTERN EUROPE | WAR IN MEDITERRANEAN AREA |
|---|---|---|---|
| 1939 | SEPT: British troops land in France | SEPT: Germany attacks Poland<br>NOV: Russia attacks Finland | |
| 1940 | APL: German invasion of Norway and Denmark<br>MAY: German invasion of Western Europe<br>JUNE: Dunkirk evacuation | MAR: Russo-Finnish Peace Treaty<br>AUG: Russians annex Baltic States | JUNE: Italians invade France<br>NOV: Italians invade Greece<br>DEC: British offensive opens in North Africa |
| 1941 | JULY: U.S. forces relieve British in Iceland<br>DEC: Germany and Italy declare war on U.S.A. | JUNE: Germany attacks Russia<br>SEPT: Leningrad besieged<br>DEC: Russian counter-attack at Moscow | JAN: British take Tobruk<br>FEB: Germans land in North Africa<br>APL: Germans invade Yugoslavia and Greece<br>MAY: Germans capture Crete |
| 1942 | AUG: Dieppe raid<br>NOV: Germans occupy Vichy France | JULY: Germans capture Sevastopol<br>SEPT: Germans attack Stalingrad<br>NOV: Russian counter-attack at Stalingrad | JUNE: Germans take Tobruk<br>OCT: Battle of El Alamein<br>NOV: Allied landings in French North Africa |
| 1943 | JAN: Casablanca Conference<br>DEC: Teheran Conference | JAN: Russians relieve Leningrad<br>FEB: Germans surrender at Stalingrad<br>JULY: Russian victory at Kursk | JAN: British enter Tripoli<br>MAY: Axis forces in North Africa surrender<br>SEPT: Allied invasion of Italy<br>Italian surrender |
| 1944 | JUNE: D-Day landings<br>JULY: Caen taken<br>DEC: German offensive in Ardennes | JAN: Leningrad completely freed by Russians<br>JULY: Russians enter Poland<br>OCT: End of Warsaw rising | MAR: Cassino destroyed<br>JUNE: Allies enter Rome<br>AUG: Allies invade S. France |
| 1945 | FEB: Yalta Conference<br>MAR: Allies cross Rhine<br>APL: Russians and Americans meet at Torgau<br>JULY: Potsdam Conference | JAN: Russians take Warsaw | |

MAY 8 GERMAN ARMED FORCES IN EUROPE SURRENDER

| WAR IN PACIFIC AREA | WAR AT SEA | WAR IN THE AIR |
| --- | --- | --- |
| | OCT: *Royal Oak* sunk<br>DEC: *Graf Spee* scuttled | |
| JUNE: Japanese occupy bases in Indo-China | FEB: *Altmark* incident<br>JULY: Royal Navy attack French Fleet at Oran<br>SEPT: British receive 50 U.S. destroyers<br>NOV: Battle of Taranto | MAY: Bombing of Rotterdam<br>AUG: ⎫<br>⎬ Battle of Britain<br>SEPT: ⎭<br>DEC: Bombing of Coventry |
| DEC: Japanese attack British, Dutch and U.S.<br>Attack on Pearl Harbour<br>Fall of Guam and Wake Island<br>Fall of Hong Kong | MAR: Battle of Matapan<br>MAY: *Bismarck* sunk<br>DEC: *Prince of Wales* and *Repulse* sunk | MAR: R.A.F. raids on Ruhr |
| JAN: Japanese invade Burma<br>FEB: Fall of Singapore<br>APL: Fall of Bataan<br>MAY: Battle of Coral Sea<br>JUNE: Midway Island Battle<br>AUG: U.S. landings on Solomons | FEB: Java Sea naval battle<br>NOV: French fleet scuttled at Toulon | MAY: First 1,000-bomber raid on Cologne |
| MAR: Battle of Bismarck Sea<br>JULY: Allied forces attack in New Guinea | SEPT: Italian fleet surrenders<br>DEC: *Scharnhorst* sunk | MAY: R.A.F. destroy Eder Moehne dams |
| FEB: Americans invade Marshall Islands<br>JUNE: Japanese retreat in Burma<br>AUG: Guam recovered | NOV: *Tirpitz* sunk | JUNE: 'V1' bombardment begins<br>SEPT: 'V2' bombardment begins<br>British airborne attack on Arnhem |
| JAN: Burma Road reopened<br>MAR: Conquest of Iwo Jima<br>JUNE: Conquest of Okinawa | | FEB: Dresden destroyed<br>AUG: Atomic bombs dropped on Hiroshima and Nagasaki |

SEPT 2 FINAL JAPANESE SURRENDER

# World War Two

*Titles in this series*

MODERN TIMES

# World War Two

C. C. Bayne-Jardine, M.A.

HENBURY COMPREHENSIVE SCHOOL, BRISTOL

LONGMAN

LONGMAN GROUP LIMITED
*Longman House,*
*Burnt Mill, Harlow, Essex CM20 2JE, England*
*and Associated Companies throughout the World*

*First published 1968*
*Twelfth impression 1985*

ISBN 0 582 20435 6

*Produced by Longman Group (FE) Ltd*
*Printed in Hong Kong*

# Preface

This brief account of World War Two is an attempt to help young people to understand the terrible and complex years, 1939–45. Obviously much has been left out of this sketch which, it is hoped, may encourage and guide further reading. I have tried to tell the story of individual courage within a framework of a technical and widespread conflict. In order to do this I have abandoned the strictly chronological approach and would ask the reader to refer to the time charts in order to get a picture of the global conflict. Perhaps it is worth calling attention to some words written in the period around 420 B.C. by Thucydides: 'That war is an evil is something that we all know, and it would be pointless to go on cataloguing all the disadvantages involved in it.'

I should like to thank all those who have helped me with this book. In particular, I should like to thank the staff of the Imperial War Museum for their great help over illustrative material and Mrs R. N. Swarbrick for drawing the maps so skilfully.

C. C. Bayne-Jardine

# Contents

*Acknowledgements*

We are grateful to the following for permission to include copyright material:

Chatto & Windus Ltd for an extract from *The Big Show* by Pierre Clostermann; Collins, Publishers, and Harcourt, Brace & World, Inc. for an extract from *The Rommel Papers* edited by B. H. Liddell Hart, copyright 1953 by B. H. Liddell Hart; Elek Books Ltd for an extract from *In Their Shallow Graves* by Zeiser (trans. Brown); Evans Brothers Ltd for an extract from *Cheshire V.C.* by Russell Braddon; Faber & Faber Ltd and Random House Inc. for an extract from 'The War God' by Stephen Spender, copyright 1942 by Stephen Spender, reprinted from *Collected Poems* (1928–53) by Stephen Spender; author's agents and author for an extract from *Operation Victory* by Sir F. de Guingand (Hodder & Stoughton); George G. Harrap and author for an extract from *A Thousand Shall Fall* by Hans Habe; George G. Harrap for an extract from *V.C's Of The Air* by J. Frayn Turner; Hutchinson Publishing for an extract from *Daedalus Returned* by Baron von der Heydte; the author for an extract from *Ball of Fire* by Antony Brett James; Peter Owen Ltd for an extract from *Children Of The A-Bomb* compiled by Dr A. Osata (1963); author's agents, author and Bodley Head for an extract from 'Missing' and an extract from 'For Johnny', both from *Collected Poems* by John Pudney; Putnam's & Coward-McCann and authors agents for an extract from *The White Cliffs* by Alice Duer Miller (1941); Simon & Schuster, Inc., and author's agents for an extract from *The War: A Concise History 1939–1945* (Robert Hale Ltd); Souvenir Press Ltd and Ballantine Books, Inc. for an extract from *The Battle of the Bulge* by Robert E. Merriam, copyright 1947 by Ziff-Davis Publishing Company under *Dark December*; and Major Elliott Viney for permission to include the anonymous poem 'Barbed Wire' which appeared in the magazine *Touchstone*, which was produced by British prisoners of war at Oflag VIIB, during 1943–45.

For permission to reproduce photographs we are grateful to the following:

Imperial War Museum—pages 35, 36, 39, 43, 45, 46, 53, 62, 67, 68, 70, 72, 73, 77, 79, 83, 84, 85, 86, 87, 88, 90, 95, 96, 99, 100, 105, 108, 110, 112, 113, 114, 115, 117, 118, 121, 123, 124, 125, 128, 130, 131, 132, 133; Keystone Press—pages 14, 32, 81, 82, 103, 133; London Express—pages 21, 57, 93, 137; Paul Popper Ltd—page 51; Radio Times Hulton Picture Library—pages 15, 31, 101; Carel Toms—page 92.

The maps on pages 25, 40, 47, 58, 109, 111 and 116 are based on some in Flower and Reeves, *The War 1939–1945*, and that on page 127 on one in Churchill, *The Second World War* Volume 3, both by permission of Cassell & Co. Ltd. The map on page 74 and diagram on page 122 are based on two in Scott-Daniell, *World War II* by permission of Ernest Benn Ltd. The cartoons by David Low are reproduced by permission of the *Evening Standard*.

# 1 The Atomic Bombs

*'War is a matter of tools, and the highest mechanical weapon nearly always wins.'*  Major-General J. F. C. Fuller, 1920

On 6 August 1945, after six years of war, the allies dropped an atomic bomb on the Japanese city of Hiroshima. This bald statement fails to catch the horror brought into the world by this weapon which killed over a period of time more than 90,000 people and injured as many more while destroying three-fifths

The smoke billowing 20,000 feet above Nagasaki after the atomic bomb had been dropped

of the city. Yoshihiro Kimura was a schoolboy in Hiroshima and his account of the explosion follows:

'We heard a voice saying, "Air raid alarm".

'I hurried home and was playing. This is because I was already used to this sort of thing. Then the alert ended and I went back to school. The teacher doesn't come so we start talking again. Pretty soon we heard a hum and saw a little aeroplane in the sky to the south-east. And this gradually grew larger and came over our heads. I was watching the aeroplane the whole time. I can't tell whether it is a foreign plane or a Japanese plane. Then suddenly a thing like a white parachute came falling. Five or six seconds later everything turned yellow in one instant. It felt the way it does when you get the sunlight straight in your eye. A second or two later, CRASH! There was a tremendous noise. Everything became dark and stones and roof tiles came pouring down on our heads. For a while I was unconscious. A whole lot of lumber came piling around my hips and I wanted to protest: "Stop, that hurts!" I came to again with the pain. I quickly crawled outside. There were lots of people lying around there; the faces of most of them were charred. I got out to the street and just as I heaved a sigh of relief my right hand suddenly began to hurt. When I looked closely at it I found that the skin of my right arm was peeled off from my elbow to my fingers and it was all red. I wanted to go

Devastation after the atomic bomb had been dropped on Hiroshima

home right away and I figured out the direction and started to walk towards the house when I heard a voice call, "Sumi-chan!" I turned and looked and it was my sister. Her clothes were torn to rags and her face was so changed that I was amazed.

'The two of us started off toward the house together but the house was flattened and there was no one there. We searched around the neighbourhood and then came back and looked and there was Father. Father was pulling off the roof and trying to get something out. But then he seemed to give that up and he came toward us.

'When I asked, "Mother?" he said tiredly, "She's dead!"'

Three days later a second bomb was dropped on Nagasaki. Group Captain Cheshire, V.C., D.S.O., D.F.C., was in the American Super-Fortress which accompanied the plane carrying the second bomb. He sat comfortably seven miles above the earth while the bomb was dropped, but even this expert bomber pilot was astounded by what followed.

'The order came to don their thick welders' glasses. The moment of history had arrived.

'When he put his glasses on, Cheshire was disconcerted and not a little annoyed to find that he could not see outside at all. Dr Penney was more patient. He knew what would follow, what they would see soon—a brilliant flash in the sky that would sear eyeballs into instant blindness, a haze of rapidly on-rushing and darkening white smoke, an instant's sound of roaring accompanied by the oppression of wind and heat . . . then oblivion.

'The scientist waited calmly while Cheshire shifted about uneasily. The bomb itself provided the answer to Cheshire's questions.

'Without warning, the warm sunlit interior of the cockpit was filled with a vicious, flaring brightness, stronger even than that of the sun itself. Every detail of the plane's interior now stood out through his welders' glasses in sharp-edged clarity. Swiftly, Cheshire turned his head to the source of this unspeakable light and was appalled.

'Over Nagasaki was a ball of fire rocketing upwards, ascending five times as fast as even the new jet aeroplanes could fly—a ball of fire miles across, billowing and malignant. Attached to it was a tail, a tail of smoke and vapour and destruction

3

which, it seemed, had torn off the very crust of the earth itself.'

This terrible weapon appalled Britain's expert bomber-pilot and brought suffering to thousands of people in Japan. It was the final product of six years' search for a knock-out weapon. On 15 August 1945 the Emperor of Japan ordered his armies to cease fighting and when the Americans landed in Japan later in the month they met with no resistance. The actual document announcing unconditional surrender by the Japanese was signed on 2 September 1945, six years and one day after Hitler's tanks had advanced into Poland. The atomic bombs had finished off World War Two.

Today many people consider that the use of such a weapon was a terrible mistake. At the time it seemed the best tool to use to force the Japanese to surrender without launching an invading army against Japan itself. Such an invasion would have meant the loss of many lives and much destruction. However, it is now clear that the Japanese were ready to surrender before the bombs were dropped provided that the Emperor's position was guaranteed by the Allies. The Allies demanded unconditional surrender and the bombs were dropped to bring this about. Six years of modern warfare had produced a weapon with a terrifying destructive potential.

The story of World War Two is the story of the great technical advances which made the manufacture of new weapons possible along with the story of great human effort and courage. People fought and suffered under desert sun, on icy oceans, in steaming jungles, under savage winter conditions and amidst the bombed ruins of their homes. This war involved the people of the world. It ended in the death-filled mushroom clouds of the atomic bombs and began when shots were fired on the Polish frontier as the German forces invaded on 1 September 1939. We must now try to find out why Germany attacked Poland in 1939.

# 2 Causes of World War Two

## The New Germany

At the end of World War One the German delegation had signed the peace treaty in the Hall of Mirrors in the Palace of Versailles on 28 June 1919. They left the ceremony with heavy hearts and with bitterness eating into them for they had been forced to accept, without discussion, full responsibility for the

Germany, 1919

war, to give up their colonies and some land in Europe, to reduce their armed forces, and to pay reparations—unspecified amounts of money to repair war damage. The bitterness felt by the Germans might well have softened if they had prospered after 1919 but, like other European countries, their nation was utterly exhausted after four years of war. Agriculture, commerce and industry were in ruins. How could Germany rebuild her economy and pay reparations to the victors? The only hope lay in renewed industries and exports. Unfortunately the Germans had no money with which to renew their factories and railways. They only managed to pay a small amount of the reparations by 1922, after a loan from Britain. In 1923 the German government stated that they could not pay any more money to the victorious powers. As a result the French occupied the mining area of the Ruhr valley where the miners promptly came out on strike. Prices in Germany soared to fantastic heights and many Germans, especially those with savings, were ruined. In November 1918 £1 exchanged for 20 German marks while in December 1923 the rate of exchange was 22,300 million marks to the pound sterling. The situation was saved by American loans and the Dawes Plan. This was a plan to pay reparations by instalments drawn up by Charles Dawes, an American banker whose slogan was, 'business not politics'. The German economy recovered only to collapse again in 1929 when the American economy crashed and American loans were called in. Under these unstable conditions the German people continued to feel bitter and to look for a strong leader to restore their wealth and their pride.

## The Guardians of the Peace

The victorious powers in 1919 were sick of war and planned for a lasting security. The League of Nations was set up so that governments could co-operate and avoid war. Unfortunately the Americans withdrew from Europe and went back to their policy of 'Isolation'. The League had no means of forcing its members to co-operate and the task of keeping the peace was really left to the two remaining great powers who had drawn up the 1919 settlement, France and Britain. The French decided to arrange for their own security against Germany and made treaties with Poland in 1921 and Czechoslovakia in 1924. In 1930 they began to strengthen their defences by building the Maginot Line, a defence line of concrete pillboxes and gun emplacements linked by underground rails. The British people faced problems of unemployment at home and wanted peace. This unwillingness to face up to the German threat and another war until the last moment is clearly shown in these lines from a contemporary poem, '*The White Cliffs*'. The speaker's husband, John, was killed in World War One and now she faces the possible loss of her son.

> Later than many, earlier than some,
> I knew the die was cast—that war must come;
> That war must come. Night after night I lay
> Steeling a broken heart to face the day
> When he, my son—would tread the very same
> Path this his father trod. When the day came
> I was not steeled—not ready. Foolish, wild
> Words issued from my lips—'My child, my child,
> Why should you die for England too?' He smiled:
> 'Is she not worth it, if I must?' he said.
> John would have answered yes—but John was dead.

In fear of another terrible war the British people closed their eyes to the German danger and their leaders failed to take any action against Hitler. Few listened to the warnings uttered by Churchill for they wanted to live in peace.

## The German Threat

The situation was made dangerous by Hitler's rise to power in Germany. The National Socialists or Nazis found in Hitler a leader and they began to exploit the bitterness and unrest in Germany. In his book *Mein Kampf* (My Struggle) Hitler claimed that the Germans had been betrayed in 1918 by the Jews and the communists. The nation was encouraged to think in terms of vengeance and a greater German empire. In 1928 Hitler wrote: 'The National Socialist movement will always let its foreign policy be determined by the necessity to secure the space necessary to the life of our people.' Hitler saw Germany as a great European power with rich agricultural colonies in the east. He turned his eyes towards Poland, the Ukraine and the borderlands of Russia and he made much of the fact that these lands were owned by Slav peoples whom he termed inferior to the German race.

By 1934 Hitler was firmly in power and the German people were enthusiastic in their support of his policy. Hitler withdrew the German delegation from the Geneva Disarmament Conference in 1933. He claimed that because the European powers would not scrap their armaments the Germans would have to rearm in spite of the 1919 Treaty. This rearmament began in 1935 and 'guns, not butter' became a national slogan.

In 1936 the powers of Europe were concentrating on containing Mussolini's actions in Abyssinia when Hitler ordered his troops to reoccupy the German Rhineland which had been

German troops march into the Demilitarised zone of the Rhineland

declared a non-military zone in 1919 and guaranteed by the Locarno Pacts of 1925. This action was a gamble and Hitler knew that he would have to withdraw if Britain and France moved against him. However, Britain and France only protested. Hitler was able to build his western wall defence line, the Siegfried Line. His western flank was defended and in the same year he gained an ally by the formation of the Berlin–Rome Axis. Later in 1936 Germany and Japan made a pact to work together against communism. Hitler now pursued his policy of expansion eastwards by using every opportunity that came his way. The Nazi party in Austria, the Germans in the

Sudeten area of Czechoslovakia and the Germans in Danzig all gave Hitler an excuse to claim territory. Britain and France wanted peace and were inclined to listen to Hitler's reasoned propaganda while Germany grew greater and more threatening to their security. Such a policy of expansion always risked an open clash.

It has been argued that Hitler did not want war in 1939 and that his plans for expansion had limits. It is possible that he made a mistake in 1939 because he believed that France and Britain would give way over Poland. It is more difficult to find any clear sign that Hitler intended to limit the size of his new German empire. The policy of the western powers until 1939 was to give way to Hitler's demands. This policy is called appeasement. Britain and France did not want war and so they listened to the careful German propaganda. There was a sense of guilt over the Treaty of Versailles in Britain and many people felt that Hitler's claims to rule over the Germans in the Rhineland and the Sudeten area of Czechoslovakia were justified. In addition it was difficult for the British and French to do anything to stop Hitler's advance in the eastern part of Europe. The only power which might halt Hitler in the East was Russia and many people in Britain and France feared Communist Russia more than they feared Hitler's Germany. In 1936 Belgium gave up her alliances and stated an official policy of neutrality. The Belgians were not alone in wishing to avoid doing anything about the moves made by Hitler.

Hitler was in a good position to take any opportunity that arose to extend the German frontiers. The Austrian Nazis were a constant threat to the existing government under von Schuschnigg and although Schuschnigg was prepared to come to terms with the Germans the Austrian Nazis forced his hand. They sent a message to Berlin asking for military assistance to put down disorder. Hitler checked that Mussolini would not move against him and then ordered his forces to march. Austria became part of the German empire. Reactions to this move were slight except among the Sudeten Germans in Czechoslovakia. Their leader, Henlein, was soon in touch with Berlin. Once again Hitler was able to use German demands in another country to support his claims for wider frontiers.

9

Hitler and Mussolini in 1938

At this point Hitler's plans received a check. The Czecho-slovakian government under President Beneš ordered their forces to mobilise in answer to threatening German troop movements. Britain, France and Russia all stated that they would support the Czechs in the event of attack. Hitler hesitated but there is little doubt that he intended to smash the Czechs before 1938 was out, whoever supported them. Throughout the summer of 1938 the tension grew and the British and French governments looked desperately for some solution other than war. In September Chamberlain, the British prime minister, met Hitler in a last minute bid for peace. Negotiations continued with meetings at Berchtesgarden, Godesberg and finally Munich.

Chamberlain spoke to the nation on the evening of 27 September 1938 before he left for Munich.

'How horrible, fantastic, incredible, it is that we should be digging trenches and trying on gas-masks here because of a quarrel in a far-away country between people of whom we know nothing.' Chamberlain went on to say: 'I am myself a man of peace to the depths of my soul. Armed conflict between nations is a nightmare to me; but if I were convinced that any nation had made up its mind to dominate the world by fear of its force I should feel that it must be resisted.' At Munich on 29 September, Hitler, Mussolini, Daladier of France and

Chamberlain reached an agreement. Germany was to have the Sudetenland and the Czech government was informed of this fact by the powers. Poland and Hungary promptly took over areas of Czechoslovakia and Hitler had got his way again. He could ignore threats against him from within Germany as long as he met with success. The agreement at Munich seemed to prove that the powers were unable to deny him his success.

## Britain and France Make a Stand

Chamberlain claimed after Munich: 'I believe it is peace for our time.' In reality he felt less hopeful after the long struggle of September 1938 and some in the cheering crowds who greeted his return were beginning to feel uneasy about German ambitions. This uneasiness became serious alarm when, in March 1939, Hitler in response to a request from some Slovakians moved into the rest of Czechoslovakia. In high glee he announced that Czechoslovakia had ceased to exist. This action forced people in Britain and France to face up to Hitler's policy. No German minority had given Hitler an excuse for this move and the attitude of the French and British began to harden against him. At the end of March 1939 Chamberlain took up a position which showed that Britain was not prepared to allow Hitler to grab Polish territory. The British government pledged support to the Poles if their independence was threatened. The French government took the same line. Feeling in the West had swung firmly against the German dictator who had so swiftly broken the Munich agreement. In Britain universal military conscription was brought in during April 1939 and Europe waited grimly for Hitler to move.

Hitler was furious at the way in which Britain and France were behaving. He shouted: 'I'll cook them a stew that they'll choke on.' He did not alter his plans for Poland. He calmly said to the Rumanian foreign minister: 'Well, if England wants war, she can have it.' The one power who could have sent military help to the Poles was Russia. The Poles feared the Russians and would not consider an alliance with them. Britain and France were also suspicious of Russian advance and so negotiations for an agreement between the three powers came to nothing. This played into the hands of the Germans. Hitler was delighted when Ribbentrop was able to sign a pact with the Russians in Moscow. This was a cynical treaty which both the Germans and the Russians knew would not last for long. The published agreement was simply that the two powers would not attack each other. With this pact there was a secret agreement on the way in which the two powers should divide eastern Europe.

Hitler was determined to regain Danzig, which lay on the Baltic at the end of the corridor of land which split East Prussia

Germany, 1939

from the rest of Germany. This corridor had been made in 1919 so that Poland should have an outlet to the sea. Hitler was determined to take back this land and was prepared to destroy Poland in the process. Late in August 1939 Hitler encouraged his generals with the words: 'I shall give a propagandist reason for starting the war, no matter whether it is plausible or not. The victor will not be asked afterwards whether he told the truth or not. When starting and waging war, it is not right that matters, but victory.'

Britain and Poland signed a formal pact on 25 August 1939

and Hitler hesitated, hoping that the powers would back down as they had done the year before at Munich. Yet he was determined to get his own way over Poland and set in motion the German attack on Poland which began on 1 September 1939.

After an angry debate in the House of Commons on 2 September the British government acted in support of Poland as they had promised. On 3 September the British ambassador demanded the withdrawal of German troops from Poland. A similar French demand followed almost at once. Hitler was silent and unmoved when he heard the news. Everything depended on the success of the German army and Goering remarked: 'If we lose this war, then God help us!' World War Two had begun. Hitler had harnessed the discontent and ambition in Germany to pursue a policy of territorial expansion. Hitler was prepared to risk a general war as he carried out his policy and the German people accepted the risk. War was the price Germany paid for Hitler's ruthless pursuit of a greater German empire.

*A summary of Hitler's moves 1934–1939*

| | | |
|---|---|---|
| 1933 | | Hitler made Chancellor of Germany |
| 1934–5 | | Germany begins to rearm. |
| 1936 | (March) | German troops move into the Rhineland area. |
| | (October) | Pact made between Germany and Italy. |
| 1938 | (March) | German occupation of Austria in support of Austrian Nazis. |
| | (September) | German occupation of part of Czechoslovakia in support of Sudeten Germans. |
| 1939 | (March) | German occupation of the rest of Czechoslovakia. |
| | (August) | Pact between Russians and Germans. |
| | (September) | German attack upon Poland launched. |

# 3 The 'Blitzkrieg'

## *The Attack on Poland*

Hitler had made careful preparations for the military move against Poland. On Wednesday, 30 August 1939 a statement of the German claims against Poland was drawn up and issued

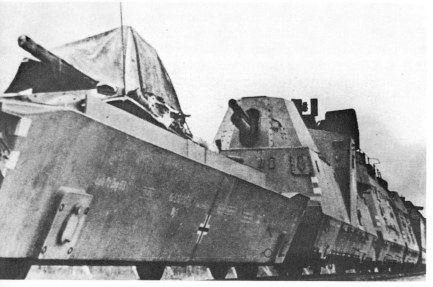

German armoured trains

under sixteen headings. The main claims were that Danzig should be returned to Germany and that the Polish Corridor should be placed under international control. The Poles were not prepared to accept German dictation and on 31 August Hitler signed 'Directive No. 1 for the Conduct of the War'.

'Case White', the attack upon Poland, was to be launched at 4.45 on 1 September while German forces in the west waited along the Siegfried Line for the French and British to make hostile moves. On the Polish frontier the S.S. moved into action. A dozen condemned criminals had been dressed in Polish uniforms and then given fatal injections. These corpses were left in the area of Gleiwitz on the Polish frontier. A few shots fired into the bodies completed the artistic scene arranged for the foreign Press who were informed of frontier incidents. The German columns moved up towards the Polish border while Berlin radio broadcast that the reasonable German requests had been violently rejected by the stubborn Poles.

At dawn on 3 September 1939 the opening shots of World War Two were fired as the German attack began. The 'Blitz-krieg' (lightning war) tactics used by the Germans took the world by surprise. The Germans used fifty-six divisions, of

A Polish farmer continues his ploughing as the German tanks move forward to attack

which nine were armoured and motorised, and concentrated their attack at selected points. The armoured spearheads swept across the open countryside in the lovely September weather. Ahead of these tank columns the German planes struck at towns and communications while behind them the German infantry fanned out and dealt with the pockets of resistance. The thirty divisions of the Polish army ready for action were spread thinly along their frontier with no reserve in support. They were soon forced back as their line was pierced by the German concentrations. Their twelve brigades of cavalry charged bravely against the German tanks but charged in vain. The Polish planes were caught on the ground and many were destroyed before they could take-off and join battle with the Germans.

During the first eight months of the war, from September 1939 to June 1940, Great Britain and France did little. Their forces were not ready to launch an attack against the German Siegfried Line and they could not get help to the Poles. As a result the western powers were static while the German forces moved at great speed.

Wilhelm Prüller was a conscript in the German army. He was determined to be a good soldier and to help in winning the new Nazi empire. He wrote in his diary for 10 September 1939.

'We're moving at a terrific pace. The roads are simply beyond description. And the Polish dead every foot. The dust is at least a foot deep. Our truck has something wrong with it. The Squadron moves on. When we get our truck going again, we hunt in vain for the Squadron for four hours.

'Our driver's mate, Hofer, again proved to be idiocy personified. We go through a large town, which our bombers had flattened out yesterday. Hours ago, our Detachment took 1,000 prisoners here. Thousands of refugees. Civilians. We move through the town. On the railway embankment you can still see Polish soldiers fleeing in the direction of Przemysel.'[1]

It is little wonder that Goering could speak to the German people and assure them that the war would be over in three or four days. The German forces converged on Warsaw and the Polish army was overwhelmed by their opponent's speed. The citizens of Warsaw made a gallant stand after the Polish government had fled to Rumania but by 27 September resistance had been crushed and Warsaw radio ceased to broadcast the Polish National Anthem. In one month the 'Blitzkrieg' had brought about the destruction of Poland.

## Russia's Advance Westward

The Russians had been surprised at the speed at which the Germans crushed the Polish forces and they hastily invaded eastern Poland on 17 September. Russians and Germans met and shook hands over a ruined Poland at Brest-Litovsk. In 1918 the Germans had dictated peace to the Russians at Brest-

[1] *Diary of a German Soldier*, by Wilhelm Prüller (Faber and Faber).

Litovsk. For the moment the new allies met at this same spot. Neither side trusted the other and Stalin was determined to push his frontier as far west as possible, to gain a barrier zone against possible German advance. On 29 September Hitler and Stalin signed the treaty partitioning Poland. Then Hitler turned his attention to the problem of his generals and their opposition to the extension of the war which they feared would prove too much for the German army to handle.

Stalin edged the Russian frontier forward. The three Baltic States of Estonia, Latvia and Lithuania were forced to admit Russian troops and became within a year Russian provinces. The Finns were also faced with a Russian demand for frontier concessions near Leningrad. The Finns refused these demands and prepared to fight along the defences of the Mannerheim Line, which commanded the approaches into Finland from Leningrad, and the snowy wastes of their eastern frontier.

The world expected a repeat of the Polish campaign. The Russians had control of the air and a large number of light tanks. On 30 November the Russians attacked at eight points along the Finnish frontier. They met with fierce resistance. A resistance encouraged by the bombing of Finnish cities. The Finns made use of the heavy snow which clogged the movements of the Russian columns. These columns were allowed to advance and then Finnish patrols cut the communications and attacked the tanks with a new hand-grenade, 'the Molotov Cocktail'.[1] The Russians were not prepared for such daring resistance and they were forced to reorganise their attack. Early in March 1940 the weight of the Russian attack told and the Finns were forced to make peace and hand over territory to Russia.

Hitler was not impressed by the Russian efforts to crush the Finns and he was encouraged to believe that he could easily defeat the Russian army. The British and the French were impressed by the gallantry of the Finns and planned to send them troops by way of Norway and Sweden. The Finns made peace before this scheme was developed but Hitler knew of it and it encouraged him to turn his attention to Norway.

[1] These were made by filling thick glass bottles with a mixture of phosphorus, naphtha and liquid rubber. This burst into flames in the air and ran down inside the turret of a tank.

17

# Denmark and Norway Fall to the Germans

The port which the Allies planned to use for a base from which to aid the Finns was Narvik. This neutral port was of vital importance to the Germans during the winter months when the Gulf of Bothnia was frozen because it was connected by rail to the Swedish iron mines. German ships used the Leads, the long corridor of Norwegian territorial waters down the coast, and so were able to collect the ore in safety. Churchill, First Lord of the Admiralty at this time, urged the government to risk infringing Norwegian neutrality in an effort to cut the German supply of ore by laying mines in the Leads. The Cabinet discussed the problem of sending troops to Narvik and from there to Finland and they discussed laying mines but they did not act. 1940 dawned and an uneasy trance lay over the western front while such problems were debated.

On 10 January a German plane on its way from Münster to Cologne made a forced landing in Belgium. A German staff officer was taken from the plane before he had burnt all his papers. These papers were found to contain the complete plan for Hitler's attack upon the western front. In fact Hitler had given out the orders for the attack on the very day that the staff officer landed in Belgium. After this incident the orders were hastily changed for it was feared that the Allies knew too much. Hitler's restless eyes were drawn back to Norway by Admiral Raeder who wanted to gain bases for German ships in Norway. Raeder was in touch with Major Quisling, a former Norwegian war minister, and assured Hitler that Quisling could arrange a rising in favour of the Germans. Hitler's uncertainty over the Norwegian scheme was dramatically ended by a daring exploit carried out by the British Navy.

The German ship, the *Altmark*, had on board the seamen captured during German raids in the south Atlantic. This ship had lain low after the sinking of the German ship, *Graf Spee*, and now slipped back into Norwegian waters on her way to Germany. She was spotted by British planes and complaints were made to the Norwegians who stated that they had searched the vessel and found no prisoners. Churchill encouraged the navy to take action. Captain Vian on the *Cossack* drew alongside the *Altmark* after the Norwegians had refused to act jointly with him. The *Altmark* tried to ram the British ship, went aground and was briskly boarded. Battened down in store-rooms and an empty oil-tank, the prisoners heard the noise on deck. Suddenly they heard British voices and the cry: 'The Navy's here!' The doors were quickly smashed down and the prisoners swarmed on deck. This action cheered the British people and also convinced Hitler that Norway must be dealt with so that he could control the sea lanes along the Norwegian coast.

In March 1940 the Finns made peace with the Russians and the Allies eventually decided to lay mines in the Leads and in the Rhine. The long period of waiting, the phoney war, seemed to be coming to an end. Early in April a British naval force set out for Narvik as a German naval force set sail for Norway.

The Germans had decided to strike and once again their blow fell with lightning speed. The German minister in Oslo had shaken members of the Norwegian government by showing them films of the conquest of Poland at a reception at the German legation. The Norwegians protested to Britain about the naval force laying mines in neutral waters. The protest was sent just as the German invasion force struck. At dawn on 9 April the Germans attacked and overran Norway's neighbour Denmark and in a matter of hours and on the same day the Germans attacked Norway.

Norway is nearly 1,000 miles long and its long sea coast meant that the naval forces could play an active part in any battle. The Germans risked a full scale clash with the British Navy and seized the key towns. Airborne troops were dropped, infantry soldiers poured out of merchant ships at Narvik where they had remained hidden, and more were landed from ships of the invasion fleet. The Norwegians were taken by surprise and, although they spurned Major Quisling, they were not prepared for war. The royal family fled, pursued by German armoured cars and only at Oslo did the German forces receive a check. There the minelayer *Olav Tryggvason* fought bravely and the skipper of a whaler which engaged the enemy lost both legs in action and then rolled overboard to die so that his men should not be disheartened. The German heavy cruiser, *Bluecher*, was also sunk by the Norwegian shore batteries and so the Germans withdrew from the direct approach to Oslo. The town was soon taken by airborne troops and landings were made lower down the coast. Within one day the Germans had taken the key towns in Norway and their main forces moved swiftly north to link with their Narvik group.

British Commandos attack a German base in Norway

The British had to act to help the Norwegians. Unlike Poland, Norway was within range. The navy was involved in a series of actions and the Germans lost ten destroyers off Narvik. However, the British found that the navy could not operate easily within range of the German Air Force. Armed landings were hastily planned. Churchill urged landings at Narvik while the Cabinet decided to send forces to Trondheim, the old capital of Norway. At one moment the admiral in command of naval forces outside Narvik was ready to attack while the general in command of the troops refused to land his force. Both men were acting in accordance with instructions. Such confusion did not make for a satisfactory action against the efficient German forces. Narvik was captured from the Germans on 28 May but, by that time, Britain was facing disaster in France and Belgium. Allied forces were finally withdrawn from Norway on 8 June and the Germans had successfully used speed and airborne forces again.

The Norwegian government and their King fled to Britain.

The British Navy had punished the German Navy in the Norwegian action so that it would not be able to cover any invasion of Britain. The effective German fleet was reduced to one cruiser, two light cruisers, and four destroyers. The British people saw in this campaign the results of the years of appeasement and they turned from Chamberlain to the man who had in fact been trying to organize the Norwegian campaign, Churchill. On 7 May at the end of the first day of the debate on the Norwegian campaign, Amery, a conservative M.P., hurled at Chamberlain the words Cromwell used to the Rump Parliament in 1654: 'Depart, I say, and let us have done with you. In the name of God, go!' On 10 May Chamberlain resigned and a coalition government was formed under the leadership of Churchill. On 13 May Churchill said to the House of Commons: 'I have nothing to offer but blood, toil, tears, and sweat. You ask, what is our policy? I will say: It is to wage war, by sea, land and air, with all our might and with all the strength that God can give us. . . .' Such a spirit was sorely needed because the Germans had attacked the western front on 10 May, the same day that Churchill took office.

**ALL BEHIND YOU, WINSTON**

A cartoon showing the spirit in which Britain greeted Churchill's appointment to office, May 1940

## *The Fall of France*

The Germans had 134 divisions facing the Allies in France and the Low Countries. The Allies had a total of 135 divisions and the French had as many tanks as the Germans, about 2,500. The difference in the two armies lay in the fact that the Germans had a single command and that the German armour was concentrated in ten panzer (tank) divisions. The Allied tanks were spread out in support of infantry units.

The 'Blitzkrieg' tactics were effective once again. The Dutch and Belgian defence systems were overrun by small groups of glider troops and parachutists who were landed on key points

The German infantry sweep through on the western front

ahead of the main forces. The great fortress of Eben Emael on the Albert Canal was captured by a glider force of 120 men armed with powerful explosives. This group landed on the roof of the fortress and blew up the guns and so put it out of action. This scheme was Hitler's own and was entirely effective. On

13 May Rotterdam was bombed and the next day the Dutch Army surrendered. Queen Wilhelmina escaped to England where the Norwegian King had already had to flee for safety.

The Allied forces including the entire British Expeditionary Force swung like a gate on a hinge at Sedan into Belgium to meet the German attack. They considered that the hinge of this move was protected by the forest area of the Ardennes. The rest of the line was firm enough behind a strong fence, the great fortifications of the Maginot Line. The Germans allowed the Allies to move forward and their planes did not harass the columns moving forward. The troops found their main obstacle on the roads were the refugees fleeing from the German bombing.

French refugees on the roads in France

The Germans prepared an armoured column over 100 miles long opposite the hinge of the Allied advance. The Ardennes proved no serious obstacle to their swift advance. The River Meuse was defended by a line of pillbox defences garrisoned by the French 9th Army, largely made up of reservists. At this defence the German armoured column struck home. The Meuse defences were bombed by planes which dived directly on their target and then released their bombs at a low level. The armour smashed through the 9th Army and were over the Meuse on 13 May.

General Rommel, the German commander of the 7th Panzer Division, wrote of his breakthrough: 'The tanks now rolled in a long column through the line of fortifications and on towards the first houses, which had been set alight by our fire. In the moonlight we could see the men of the 7th Motor-cycle Battalion moving forward on foot beside us. Occasionally an enemy machine-gun or anti-tank gun fired, but none of their shots came anywhere near us. Our artillery was dropping heavy harassing fire on villages and the road far ahead of the regiment. Gradually the speed increased. Before long we were five hundred—a thousand—two thousand—three thousand yards into the fortified zone. Engines roared, tank tracks clanked and clattered. Whether or not the enemy was firing was impossible to tell in the ear-splitting noise. We crossed the railway line a mile or so south-west of Solre le Château, and then swung north to the main road which was soon reached. Then off along the road and past the first houses.

'The people in the houses were rudely awoken by the din of our tanks, the clatter and roar of tracks and engines. Troops lay bivouacked beside the road, military vehicles stood parked in farmyards and in some places on the road itself. Civilians and French troops, their faces distorted with terror, lay huddled in the ditches, alongside hedges and in every hollow beside the road. We passed refugee columns, the carts abandoned by their owners, who had fled in panic into the fields. On we went, at a steady speed, towards our objective. Every so often a quick glance at the map by a shaded light and a short wireless message to Divisional H.Q. to report the position and thus the success of the 25th Panzer Regiment. Every so often a look out of the hatch to assure myself that there was still no resistance and that contact was being maintained to the rear. The flat countryside lay spread out around us under the cold light of the moon. We were through the Maginot defences!'

The hinge of the allied advance was broken and the map shows how the Germans had caught the British Army and the

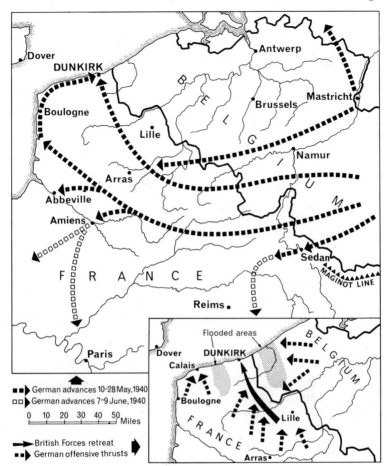

The retreat to Dunkirk before the German attack

best French divisions in a trap. On 20 May the Germans reached the mouth of the Somme at Abbeville. A week later the Belgian King commanded his forces to stop fighting and the German tanks raced towards the last escape-port open to the trapped armies. The 'Blitzkrieg' had succeeded beyond Hitler's expectations and he hesitated.

The German tanks halted a few miles south of Dunkirk on 24 May for forty-eight hours. During this time the British were able to strengthen their defences and so make an evacuation possible. The reasons for this halt are not clear. The Germans

25

probably considered that the British were finished and that they would make peace when the French were defeated. Goering claimed that the 'Luftwaffe', the German air force, could destroy British forces on the beaches and in any case Hitler wished to preserve his precious tanks for later actions. The Dunkirk perimeter was held and the evacuation made possible by this delay and by the gallant rearguard action fought under Brigadier Nicholson at Calais. The French in Lille under General Molinie also held seven German divisions for four days before being forced to surrender and so allow even more weight to be placed upon the Dunkirk beach and its ring of defenders.

British, French and Belgian soldiers wait on the beach at Dunkirk

Operation 'Dynamo' was now set in action by the British admiralty and Churchill has described the result.

'Everyone who had a boat of any kind, steam or sail, set out for Dunkirk, and the preparations, fortunately begun a week earlier, were now aided by the brilliant improvisation of volunteers on an amazing scale. The numbers arriving on the 29th were small, but they were the forerunners of nearly four hundred small craft which from the 31st were destined to play a vital part by ferrying from the beaches to the off-lying ships almost a hundred thousand men. In these days I missed the head of my Admiralty Map Room, Captain Pim, and one or two other familiar faces. They had got hold of a Dutch 'schuit' which in four days brought off eight hundred soldiers. Altogether there came to the rescue of the Army under the ceaseless air bombardment of the enemy about eight hundred and sixty

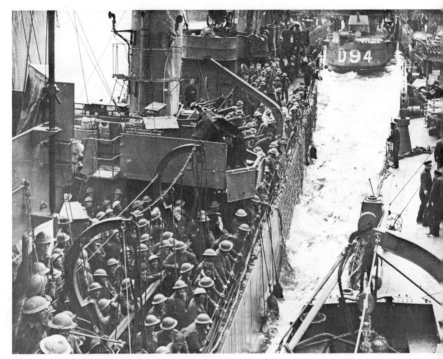

Troops on a transport at Dover

vessels, of which nearly seven hundred were British and the rest Allied.'

The weather remained fine and on 3 June 1940 the last of the 338,226 men taken off from Dunkirk clambered on board a rescue ship. Almost the entire B.E.F. and nearly 140,000 French troops had been saved, though all the army's heavy equipment, six destroyers, and 474 aeroplanes had been lost in the process. The Germans did not wait to study the equipment littering the beaches around Dunkirk. They turned their attention against the remaining armies in France. On 5 June they attacked and by 14 June Paris had fallen. The French armies fell apart.

Hans Habe has described the chaos of the fighting in France.
'When I went out of the church with Kohn Gabriel I heard
the first German tanks entering the town.

'The panic had started while we were inside. Soldiers ran
up and down in the square looking for cover. There were
practically no officers left; at least none appeared in the square.
Even today I believe that some of the men lost their minds at
this moment. I still can see Sergeant Rupin dashing madly
about the square on his bicycle, round and round, like a partici-
pant in a six-day cycle race. Again and again he flitted by my
nose, and I couldn't stop him. Adjutant Lesfauries stumbled
by me asking, with an infinitely stupid look, whether there was

Europe after one year of war, 1940

anything new. He did not wait for my answer. Some lay flat on the pavement, pressing their guns to their shoulders. This gesture—only natural on the battlefield—here seemed grotesque. Men with rifles, with knapsacks on their backs, lay on the pavements of the main square like toy soldiers on the carpet of a nursery. The first planes appeared. We could no longer distinguish between the sound of the planes and the tanks. A bomb fell in the middle of the square. Stones hurtled through the air. You could hardly tell whether it was day or night. Each bomb that fell spread light and then darkness.'

General Sir Alan Brooke was authorised to save the last two British divisions. The 51st Division was lost because fog held up evacuation but just over 190,000 men were brought off from France at this time. Reynaud, the leader of the French government, resigned on 16 June and Marshal Pétain formed a government and asked the Germans for an armistice. This was concluded on 22 June. France had fallen to the 'Blitzkrieg' and Hitler took savage joy in signing this armistice in the same railway restaurant car, brought from a Paris museum, which had been used for the armistice on 11 November 1918 when Germany surrendered to the Allies at the end of World War One.

# 4 The Battle of Britain

## Invasion Threat 1940

'What General Weygand called the Battle of France is over. I expect that the Battle of Britain is about to begin. Upon this battle depends the survival of Christian civilisation.' In these words Churchill addressed a solemn House of Commons on 18 June 1940 after the collapse of France. He ended his speech with the words: 'Let us therefore brace ourselves to our duties, and so bear ourselves that, if the British Empire and its Commonwealth lasts for a thousand years, men will still say: "This was their finest hour".'

The French were defeated. Pétain set up a government in Vichy and made terms with the Germans who occupied northern France. Only General de Gaulle kept the French flag flying with his organisation of the Free French forces from London. The Germans turned their full attention to Britain which lay across the narrow waters of the English Channel. The German armoured forces could only get to Britain if their navy could hold the Channel. The German Navy claimed that they could hold a corridor across the Channel provided that they had full air support. It was vital to German plans that the British Air Force should be destroyed. Once control of the air had been gained the German Air Force could support the ships and barges of the invasion force. These ships and barges were laboriously collected together over the summer of 1940. The army and navy leaders told Hitler that the launching of operation 'Sea Lion', the invasion of Britain, depended upon the success of the German Air Force.

Preparations took time and the German leaders set 15 September as the earliest possible date for invasion. During the summer months of 1940 Britain made what preparations she could to meet the German threat. The Royal Navy acted speedily to stop the French fleet falling into German hands. Most French ships in British ports and at Alexandria gave way or joined the British forces. At Oran the French officers resented British claims and, under strict orders from London, Sir James Somerville, the British admiral, was forced to open fire and destroy two French battleships and a battlecruiser. Britain kept control of the sea at the expense of her ally.

At home elaborate precautions were taken to make the German advance difficult. Road signs were removed and station place names painted out or taken down. Huge anti-tank ditches were dug across south-east England and you can still find concrete anti-tank blocks overgrown with weeds and wild

The Home Guard on the terrace at County Hall, August 1940

flowers in the English countryside. The Local Defence Volunteers had been formed at the beginning of the French campaign. They were now renamed the Home Guard and, armed with a strange array of weapons from homemade pikes to shotguns, they prepared to 'take one with them' as they died. Churchill halted the evacuation of families overseas and King George VI practised revolver shooting in the grounds of Buckingham Palace, where he was prepared to die.

31

The Home Guard prepares to 'take one with them'

Beaverbrook, as minister of aircraft production, turned his full energies to increasing the production of fighter aircraft. Iron railings, aluminium pans, and all scrap metal went towards the frenzied production of fighters. The British knew as well as the Germans that their survival would depend on the coming battle for control of the air. Air Marshal Dowding had refused to allow more British aeroplanes to be sent to France early in the year in spite of Churchill's wishes. As a result he had fifty-five squadrons of fighters, mostly Spitfires and Hurricanes, ready to defend Britain. There were only about 1,500 trained pilots for these planes but they were helped by knowing when the enemy were approaching. This vital knowledge came from the chain of radar stations which was in full working order by this time.

## Battle over England

The weather remained fine during the summer of 1940 while British and German planes fought in the skies over the southern counties of England. On 16 August 1940, Flight Lieutenant James Nicholson of 249 Squadron raced to his Hurricane in

Pilots answer the 'scramble' signal

answer to a scramble signal. His plane roared along the runway and hurtled into the warm summer air. Over Southampton Nicholson engaged the enemy fighters escorting bombers on a daylight raid.

Nicholson swung his Hurricane at 300 miles an hour to engage a Messerschmitt. Before he could open fire the German fighter fired four cannon-shells into his Hurricane. Nicholson himself was hit in one eye and a foot. His plane's engine stuttered and the petrol tank burst into flames. The airscrew fanned the flames and the Hurricane began to blaze like a bonfire. Nicholson opened his cockpit hood and prepared to bale out. Just as he stood up he saw the enemy plane in front of him so he dropped back into his fiery cockpit and struggled to position his plane. He waited until the range was certain and then pressed the firing-button. The Messerschmitt spun away and crashed into the ground while the blazing Hurricane flew on.

Once again Nicholson struggled out of the cockpit and flung himself clear of his plane. He parachuted to the ground and was found just outside Southampton. He was rushed to hospital suffering from his wounds and terrible burns. For two days his life hung in the balance and then gradually he began to recover. For this action he was awarded the Victoria Cross; the only fighter pilot to win this award. Unfortunately Nicholson was killed in 1945 when his Liberator crashed in the Bay of Bengal. His brave action as he fought an isolated battle over the south coast of England in 1940 was symbolic of the gallantry of the fighter pilots in the Battle of Britain.

Such lone actions were controlled by the pulsing heart of the Group Operations Room. At Uxbridge, fifty feet below ground,

Air Vice-Marshal Parks commanded number 11 Group. His staff sifted the information from the radar stations and from the observers stationed at various points to give information about the course of the enemy planes overhead. Lights flashed to indicate squadron readiness and discs were pushed to and fro on a large map-table to show the battle situation. In this way the battle could be controlled, planes refuelled in turn, and the most made of slender resources. The anti-aircraft batteries also reported in to this operations room and so their fire power could also be geared into the defence system.

The German fighters and bombers pounded in vain against this efficient system and the gallant fighter pilots. The Germans reckoned that the Battle of Britain began on 13 August when they switched from bombing convoys of merchant ships to a full attack on south-east England. Squadrons of bombers swept over England protected by umbrellas of fighters. The British attacked the bombers and by 18 August the Germans had lost 236 aeroplanes against 95 British. The Germans then switched their attack to the fighter bases and the position began to look grim for Britain. Between the end of August and 6 September losses were more equal; 225 German aeroplanes were shot down against 185 British and the disruption of British fighter bases was almost completed. Then on 7 September the Germans turned from the fighter bases in Kent and began to bomb London. Hitler reckoned that such an attack would break the British spirit and would be retaliation for the British bombing of German towns. The attacks intensified and invasion was expected at any moment. During August the bodies of about forty German soldiers had been washed up on the English Channel coast. They had been drowned while practising landing from barges in France. The tides would be right for invasion early in September and the country was alerted for German landings. In some places the church bells were rung as warning of German attack and then nothing happened.

The 'Luftwaffe' made its supreme effort on 15 September and lost fifty-six planes against twenty-six British. The British press claimed that 185 German aeroplanes had been shot down but even the true figure was enough to halt the German plans. They had failed to gain control of the air and on 17 September Hitler postponed the invasion. Great Britain had been saved

A German Focke-Wulf 190 fighter blows up under fire from a Hawker Typhoon. These aircraft came into operation at a later stage of the war

from the 'Blitzkrieg' and Churchill paid tribute to the R.A.F. in the famous words: 'Never in the field of human conflict was so much owed by so many to so few.'

# 5 Desert Warfare 1940—43

## *The First Libyan Campaign, 1940–41*

The North African desert is flat and silent. The sand stretches on and on into the distance and one clear, hot, cloudless day follows another. Apart from the light morning breeze the only wind that blows is the Khamseen. This dry wind may blow for days and it picks up the fine desert sand until a huge yellow dust-cloud billows over the land. Visibility is cut to a few yards and sand creeps into every nook and cranny. The Bedouins muffle their heads in rags and patiently sit out such storms. European troops learnt that even war had to stop for the Khamseen. They also learnt that war in the desert was very like war at sea. Groups went out into the unknown on compass bearings and swept over the sands searching for the enemy. Mobility was the key to desert warfare. Commonwealth soldiers learnt to thrive on tinned foods and a gallon of water a day, in the blazing heat which made it possible for a tank commander to fry eggs on the steel roof of his tank. These military nomads were at their weakest when their supply lines were longest and so the fortunes of war in the desert swung backwards and forwards as first one side then the other extended their supply lines.

All vehicles could be seen moving from afar because of the trail of dust that billowed up behind or to one side

'All vehicles could be seen moving from afar because of the trail of dust that billowed up behind or to one side. When two trucks did meet, each driver tried desperately to steer to windward and so avoid the dust of the other vehicle. You might wear sand-goggles but your face was coated with sand that caked itself into a beige mask, clinging to the sweat of your countenance, collecting in the corners of your eyes. Hands and arms, necks and knees became coated with this same sand, which penetrated under your shirt, and caught in your throat, and made your eyes smart. Your hair became matted and bistre. Along your limbs the trickling sweat would cleave little rivulets through the sandy coating.

'All day long thousands of vehicles shod with balloon tyres or with tracks were moving about, each with its plume of sand that poured up over the mudguards, penetrated into the carburettor, came through chinks in the truck's body, or round the edge of a staff car's windows. The tanks cut deep ruts in the sand. Half the surface of the desert might appear to be in the air at one time, and drivers would keep their windscreen-wipers going in order to clear the dust and so see a few yards ahead.'

This account of conditions in the desert continues with a paragraph about the vital importance of water.

'Although you were permanently coated with sand when driving or when the wind blew up, baths were impossible and you grew accustomed to being dirty, to washing seldom. Water was short in the desert, scarcer by far than petrol. On a gallon a day for all purposes it became an art to wash, shave, clean your teeth, wash your feet, all in a mug of water, with the resultant glutinous fluid being strained and poured into the radiator of your truck.'

In the summer of 1940 Mussolini saw his great chance to drive the British out of North Africa and make the Mediterranean an Italian lake. The Italians had large forces in Africa and the British not only faced invasion by the Germans at home but also faced being driven from Egypt by the Italians. General Wavell, the British commander in the Middle East, had less than 90,000 troops and little modern equipment with which to save the situation. In any case all shipping to Egypt, India and the Far East had to take the long route round the Cape of Good Hope, for during the years 1940–43 Britain was in no position

The Mediterranean area, 1939

to protect the Suez canal route. The situation looked black for the British and an Italian medal was struck to mark the triumphal entry of Mussolini into Egypt.

Wavell made his plans calmly and secretly. The Italians, numbering over 400,000, probed into Egypt, the Sudan and Kenya. British Somaliland was abandoned in the face of their advance but in September Wavell received a precious cargo. In spite of the invasion threat from the Germans in France Churchill had ordered fifty heavy tanks to be sent to Wavell. These tanks formed the heart of what Wavell termed an 'important raid' which was launched against the Italians in December, 1940. On the morning of 9 December Wavell called the Cairo war correspondents to his office and smiling slightly told them: 'We have attacked in the Western Desert.' This raid against the Italian positions was so successful that it was turned into a full scale attack. The coastal fortress towns of Bardia and Tobruk fell in January 1941. In two months the swiftly moving British forces surprised the Italians in their camps and defence positions and took over 114,000 prisoners. Confusion lowered the morale of the Italians. A company of Australians arrived on Derna aerodrome and settled down for the night. In the morning they discovered a powerful section of Italian tanks with the crews cooking breakfast. The Australians called up artillery support and the Italian tanks were destroyed before the surprised crews had finished their break-

Australian Bren carriers moving up in battle formation towards Bardia

fasts. Wavell's forces pushed on along the coast of Libya as the winter weather turned this route into mud and slush under the wheels and tracks of their transport.

Elsewhere in Africa the Allies met with mixed fortunes. The Free French under General de Gaulle were determined to play their part in halting the spread of German and Italian influence. They resented the way in which the government of Vichy France went along with Germany. For their part the Vichy government were determined to avoid open war so they were careful not to join Germany openly against Britain. In Liverpool the Free French forces received tropical kit and at a dinner a group of officers raised their glasses and toasted 'Dakar'. A Franco-British plan had been made to land the Free French at Dakar and so take a naval base from Vichy control. Vichy forces raced to the spot and the landing failed. However, General de Gaulle's forces went on to take Duala in the Cameroons and so control French Equatorial Africa. The map also shows how this helped the later development of an air transport route across Africa. This action took place late in September 1940 and early in 1941 Wavell's forces overran Italian East Africa. The other Middle-East areas in which Allied forces were involved were Iraq and Syria. In May 1941 British forces entered Iraq to defeat the pro-German government of Rashid Ali, while in July 1941 Free French and British forces drove the Vichy government out of Syria and the Lebanon.

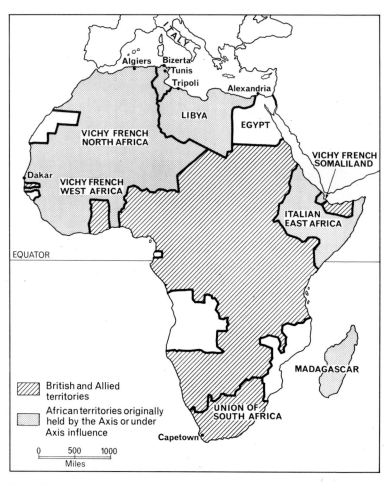

The African war area

Wavell's advancing troops were halted in Libya for political reasons. The Italians had invaded Greece from Albania late in 1940. The Greeks held the Italian attack and began a counter-attack while the Germans turned their attention to the Balkans. German soldiers had moved into Rumania to protect the oil fields and Hungary and Bulgaria joined the German alliance. The government of Yugoslavia also made an alliance with Germany but this action led to a popular re-

The German attack in the Balkans

bellion in the name of the young King, Peter II. The streets of Belgrade were filled with people singing and dancing and British and French flags flew everywhere. Hitler did not consider such rebellion to be a joke for the Yugoslavs could take the Italian army in Albania in the rear. On 6 April 1941 German bombers swept over Belgrade and pounded the city for three days. The city was smashed and, after the bombing, a bear from the city zoo wandered sadly through the ruins down to the Danube. Like the people of Yugoslavia he failed to understand what had happened.

The Germans swept on through the Balkans and into Greece in support of the Italians. Churchill had promised to support the Greeks and Wavell was ordered to send help. This was the point at which his desert advance was halted. The German

'Blitzkrieg' struck again. This time they swept over the Bulgarian frontier into Greece. Airborne troops were used skilfully and seized such key points as the bridge over the Corinth Canal. British troops were withdrawn and on 27 April 1941 the Germans entered Athens. A large force of Australian, New Zealand and British soldiers remained in Crete. The Germans used their control of the air to take the island by airborne assault. For the first time an island was taken from the air while the defenders still had control of the sea.

A German officer has described the tense excitement of this great attack from the air.

'I was aroused by my adjutant and started awake, still drowsy, to hear a roar of engines growing louder and louder, as if coming from a great distance. It took me a moment or two to remember where I was and what lay before me.

'"We are nearing Crete, sir."

'I got up and moved towards the open door beside which the dispatcher, whose duty it was to see that all final preparations for the jumps were ready, was seated. Our plane was poised steady in the air, almost as though motionless. Looking out, beyond the silver-grey wing with its black cross marking, I could see our target—still small, like a cliff rising out of the glittering sea to meet us—the island of Crete.

'Slowly, infinitely slowly, like the last drops wrung from a drying well, the minutes passed. Again and again I glanced stealthily at my wristwatch. There is nothing so awful, so exhausting, as this waiting for the moment to jump. In vain I tried to compel myself to be calm and patient. A strange unrest had also gripped most of those who were flying with me.'

Before long the pilot ordered: 'Prepare to jump!' and the officer continued his account: 'Everyone rose and started to fasten his hook to the static line which ran down the centre of the body of the plane. And while we stood there, securing our hooks, we noticed that we were losing height, and the pressure of air became hard, almost painful, to the ear.'

Next came the order, 'Ready to jump!'

'In two strides I was at the door, my men pressing close behind me, and grasped the supports on either side of it. The slipstream clutched at my cheeks, and I felt as though they were fluttering like small flags in the wind.'

German parachute troops landing on Crete. The leader of the section has a white parachute

The plane slowed down and the Germans jumped and took the island of Crete from the air.

## Germans Intervene in Africa, 1941

Wavell's advance along the coast had been halted while help was sent to Greece. In April 1941 the Germans sent help to the Italians who had been driven back by Wavell. A new figure appeared on the scene in the desert. The German general, Erwin Rommel, became part of the legend of desert warfare. Rommel proved himself to be a master in handling the mobile

General Erwin Rommel in the desert, February 1942

forces which could have such astonishing success in the desert. He won a tribute from Churchill as 'a great general' and died in 1944 for his part in the plot to overthrow Hitler. Now he launched his attack and the British fell back. Only Tobruk held out in Rommel's rear and his advance halted on the Egyptian border. The garrison in Tobruk held out all through the summer of 1941. Supplies came in from the sea and the Australian garrison proved their skill and courage as they perfected their defences and used all available resources. The cooks and orderlies set up a number of pre-war guns and fired them off effectively in support of the artillery batteries. The 'rats of Tobruk' showed the Germans that they could bite.

Churchill felt that Wavell was tiring under the strain of the campaign and so he arranged that Wavell should go to India and the commander there, General Auchinleck, should take his place in the desert. On 11 December 1941 Auchinleck attacked and Rommel, whose reserves had been weakened to send help to the Russian front, fell back. Tobruk was relieved and the British forces reached a point just short of El Agheila where Wavell's troops had halted the year before. At this time the main German interest lay in Russia and the raids of the British long range desert groups confirmed this. These groups, which travelled light and fast and which struck deep into the enemy lines, often captured letters written home by German soldiers. Again and again these letters were full of the news from the Russian front and questions about that front.

However, Hitler was not prepared to see Rommel defeated for lack of supplies. The Germans concentrated on sending him reinforcements. Malta, which threatened the supply route, was pounded mercilessly. The British lost the aircraft carrier *Ark Royal* among other ships in this attack and Rommel received his supplies. In May 1942 Rommel struck. His forces swept over the desert, captured Tobruk, and were within seventy miles of Alexandria when they were checked. The Germans were well equipped. The 'jerry can' proved a better container for water and petrol than the British four gallon drums which easily burst. The German tank weapons out-ranged the British and their technical organisation was superb. Once again things looked black for the British but Rommel had stretched his communications to the limit.

## *Desert Victory 1942–43*

British forces now occupied the forty-mile gap between the impassable Qattara Depression in the desert and the coast in the area of El Alamein. They were strengthened by the arrival of 300 American Sherman tanks and the command was changed again. General Alexander became the commander in the Middle East while General Montgomery took over command of the Eighth Army. General Gott had been selected for this post. He had made a great name for himself in the desert but was killed when his aircraft was shot down. Montgomery was now to make his name in the desert. Swiftly he arranged defence positions and carefully encouraged the spirit of the Eighth Army, the Desert Rats. His sharp features beneath his Australian hat studded with badges became well known as he moved about his new command.

General Montgomery wearing his Australian hat studded with the badges of the Eighth Army

Montgomery made the most of the strong defensive position which he held and Rommel's attack beat in vain against the Alam Halfa ridge. Rommel drew back and Montgomery built up his resources for an attack. In his caravan he pinned up three quotations, one of which was taken from Shakespeare's *Henry V*: 'O God of battles! steel my soldiers' hearts.' On the night of 23 October the mettle of the soldiers was tested as the Battle of Alamein began. The British attack punched home after a tremendous artillery barrage. Montgomery lost more tanks than the enemy but they had scant reserves and were hammered into retreat.

A 25-pounder gun moves up into action in tne desert

Montgomery's Chief of Staff has described the decisive phase of the battle.

'For most of the day, the two German Panzer divisions launched attacks against our Kidney Hill positions. This suited us well, and the 1st Armoured Division excelled themselves. They claimed fifty enemy tanks knocked out, as well as others damaged. In addition, the R.A.F. was doing good work bombing these attacks as they formed up. Good claims of transport destroyed were made. It was an exciting day, and during the afternoon I stood by our command vehicle listening to the loud-speaker which was turned to the wireless "net" which served the forward tanks. We heard a running commentary on the fight. One could hear the fire orders being given to the tank crews and the results of their shooting. This sort of thing:

' "Look out, Bob, a couple sneaking up your right flank—you should see them any moment now."

'You would hear the fire order given by the tank commander as the enemy came into view. Then:

' "Well done—good shooting—another brew-up."

'We ticked off the numbers claimed and felt very pleased. Looking westward there were visible signs of success. Pillars of black smoke towering into the sky showed the truth of the reports we were hearing on the radio.'

On the other side of the battlefield Rommel snatched a few moments to write to his wife.

'Dearest Lu,

Who knows whether I'll have a chance to sit down and write in peace in the next few days or ever again. Today there's still a chance.

'The battle is raging. Perhaps we will still manage to be able to stick it out, in spite of all that's against us—but it may go wrong and that would have very grave consequences for the whole course of the war. For North Africa would then fall to the British in a few days, almost without a fight. We will do all we can to pull it off. But the enemy's superiority is terrific and our resources very small . . .'

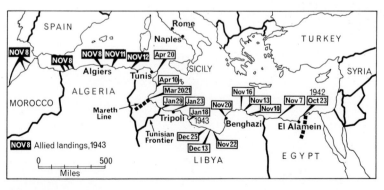

North Africa, 1942–43

On 8 November 1942 Anglo-American forces under Eisenhower's command landed in French North Africa. Part of this force crossed the Atlantic, dodging enemy submarines and fuelling from tankers, in order to make landings round Casablanca. Rommel was caught in a great Allied pincer movement. He took up a defensive position in Tunis along the Mareth Line but, in spite of reinforcements sent over by Hitler, Rommel's position was doomed. In May 1943 the combined Allied armies under Eisenhower took Tunis and a quarter of a million prisoners. The German and Italian forces had been driven out of Africa after three years of desert warfare.

# 6 Germany's Second Front Against the Russians

## *The German Attack, June–December 1941*

'We have only to kick in the door and the whole rotten structure will come crashing down.' In these words Hitler spoke confidently of the destruction of Russia. Since his early years when he formulated his ideas in *Mein Kampf* Hitler had been determined to push the German frontier eastwards. He believed that Russia would collapse as France had done and the showing made by Russian forces against Finland encouraged him in this belief. The German 'Blitzkrieg' would destroy the Red Army and then the Germans would take over an area up to a rough line from Leningrad down the Volga to the Caspian Sea. The Russians would be driven behind the Urals and out of Europe and when Germany held these new lands she would be strong enough to defy any attack and certainly strong enough to finish off Britain. This was Hitler's general plan. He decided to attack Russia before the Battle of Britain was fought and regardless of the outcome of that battle he determined 'to smash Russia'. Colonel Von Kleist was perhaps more realistic than Hitler when he pointed out: 'The German army in fighting Russia is like an elephant attacking a host of ants. The elephant will kill thousands, perhaps even millions, but in the end their numbers will overcome him, and he will be eaten to the bone.'

Stalin refused to believe that Hitler would attack in 1941 and kept his army near the frontier and played for time. He even agreed to supply Germany with oil and grain in January 1941. Yet all the time Hitler was determined to destroy Germany's great Slav neighbour who stood for communism. On 18 December 1940 Hitler issued directions for 'Operation Barbarossa'. This was the code name for the 'quick campaign' against

49

Russia to start in May 1941. Less than a week earlier Hitler had issued orders for 'Operation Marita' for an attack upon Greece. The operations in the Balkans and the landing on Crete proved to be an important diversion. The Germans were successful in the Balkans (page 41) but 'Operation Barbarossa' had to be delayed until June 1941. This delay left little time for the German advance to reach its objectives before the Russian winter set in.

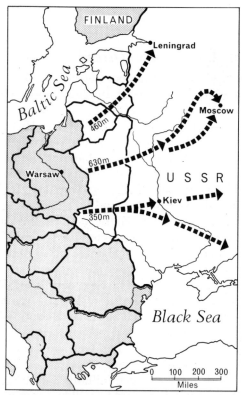

The German invasion of Russia

On 22 June 1941 the Germans invaded Russia. Exactly 129 years earlier Napoleon had invaded Russia with his Grand Army only to be defeated by the wide open spaces of Russia and the Russian winter. Now Hitler's army struck and covered hundreds of miles as they swept into Russia. The German Army formed the heart of the attacking force but Hitler had gathered in allies. The Finns were hoping to get back the land they had lost to the Russians and joined the attack. Hungary, Rumania and Italy sent troops and Spanish volunteers also joined the army which totalled over three million men. The spearheads of the invasion were made up from seventeen armoured divisions and thirteen motorised divisions. These spearheads struck for Leningrad in the north, Moscow in the centre and Stalingrad and the Caucasus in the south.

The Germans attack in the Moscow area

At first the German 'Blitzkrieg' was successful. The 'Luftwaffe' won control of the air after destroying a large number of Russian planes on the ground and German tanks sliced deep into Russian territory. The army group in the north reached Leningrad on 8 September and laid siege to the city. The centre force reached Smolensk by 7 August but had to pause there after fierce fighting. The southern strike began in July, encircled 700,000 Russians in Kiev, and reached Rostov on 21 November. Hitler was triumphant and exclaimed: 'Russia is broken! She will never rise again.'

The Russians withdrew sullenly from the punch of the 'Blitz-krieg'. Stalin called for a scorched earth policy and the people of Russia responded. The great power station on the Dnieper was dynamited on 28 August 1941 and Kiev was systematically destroyed before the Germans took it. Only the independent Ukranians welcomed the Germans as liberators from Stalin's rule yet Hitler treated them so harshly that their initial welcome turned to grim hatred.

On 2 October 1941 Hitler issued an Order of the Day to his soldiers. 'Today begins the last great decisive battle of the year'. His army had moved 400 miles into Russia and the capital, Moscow, was only 200 miles ahead. In spite of the poor roads and the problem caused by the changing of the Russian broad gauge railway track to fit German trucks, Hitler was deter-mined that the attack should go on to Moscow. The German generals wanted to concentrate the attack but Hitler was determined to continue the push in the north and the south as well. General Von Bock's army in the centre closed on Moscow, which was not only the capital of the U.S.S.R. but also the key to the railway system. In three weeks the Germans were within seventy miles of the city. The Russian government moved to the east while Stalin calmly remained in the Kremlin and ordered the Russian forces to concentrate round their capital.

In November 1941 the weather changed and the Russian winter began to close in. The Germans made one last effort to take Moscow and on 2 December 1941 their advance troops reached the suburbs.

A group of Germans reached a tram-stop on the edge of Moscow: 'There was a deathly silence all round. In front of us lay the tramway shelter and the telegraph poles silently pointed the way to the great city beyond the curtain of snow.

'"Let's walk across and have a look at that tramway station," Kagenck said. "Then we can tell Neuhoff that we were only a tram ride from Moscow."

'We walked silently down the road to the stone shed. There was not a movement around us as we stopped and stared at the wooden seats on which thousands of Muscovites had sat and waited for the tram to clang down the road from Moscow.

'There was an old wooden bin attached to one wall. I felt inside and dragged out a handful of old tram tickets. We picked out the cyrillic letters, which by now we knew spelled "Moskva".

'Slowly we trudged back to the car. Kagenck broke the silence and spoke for both of us: "It must fall, yet . . . I wonder . . ."

'Fischer turned the car round and we headed back along the white road.

'The snow was falling a little more heavily now.'

Then the winter weather halted the German armies, unprepared for the terrible conditions. Tank crews had to keep fires burning beneath the engines of tanks to stop them freezing completely. The Germans had been issued with boots that fitted them exactly and so they could not wear more than one pair of socks. Thousands suffered from frostbite and thousands suffered hunger as the supply trucks slithered to a halt.

The Russians prepared to fight back. In Moscow a foreign correspondent reported: "In all small shops which were not evacuated, work was turned entirely to war orders. One, which had been making pots and pans, started turning out hand grenades. Another, which usually made cash registers and adding machines, began producing automatic rifles.' Leningrad refused to give in. The city was almost encircled in November 1941 but the Russians kept open a single road access across the ice of Lake Ladoga. The city was held in a grim fight which lasted for sixteen months. Then, the day before the Japanese attack on Pearl Harbour, the Russians under Marshal Zhukov attacked the Germans round Moscow. The Germans were

Russian soldiers counter-attack

ordered not to retreat by Hitler and the entry from a soldier's diary for Christmas Eve 1941 shows the savage conditions of this fight: 'Day after day, night after night, we sit in the open air, and a rain of artillery and small arms fire pours over us. We think our feet will freeze at any moment. And we've no real billets. We are standing(!)—30 of us—in a room 3 × 5 metres. No windows. Nor can we heat the place, lest the smoke discloses our whereabouts. But our men—they go on standing. They can't be beaten. It is an act of heroism even greater than that of the World War. It is the most fabulous epoch of German soldiery.'

The Germans were pushed back but their line held. Berlin radio had announced that the eastern attack had halted because of the weather. For the soldiers at the front the fight became one for survival. They drew in to a series of defensive blocks or 'hedgehogs' and these were supplied by air transport. In this way the Germans held on through the winter of 1941–42.

## New Allies

The Russians expected help in their battle against Germany and Churchill responded by stating: 'Any man or state who fights against Nazism will have our aid.' By 13 July 1941 Great Britain and Russia had signed a mutual aid treaty. Germany now faced Britain and Russia but Hitler was certain of victory and, when Japan attacked the United States' base at Pearl Harbour on 7 December 1941, he cheerfully declared war on the U.S.A. He had hoped that Japan would attack in this way and expected them to move against Russia as well. This the Japanese did not do for they had learnt not to trust Hitler who never told his allies about his own plans. Hitler casually added the United States to the ranks of his enemies and Mussolini followed suit.

The Japanese attack brought the United States fully and openly into a war towards which they had been drifting slowly. In September 1939 President Franklin D. Roosevelt of the United States had issued a proclamation of neutrality. However, a system of 'cash and carry' was approved by Congress in November 1939. Any power could buy arms from the U.S.A. for cash and carry them away in their own ships. Obviously Britain with her navy was the power to benefit from this.

Roosevelt's sympathies were with Britain and in September 1940 he arranged a deal under which fifty over-age American destroyers were given to Britain in return for a ninety-nine year lease of certain naval and air bases. This action was taken without reference to Congress for the isolationists were still powerful and were determined to keep out of war. By April 1941 more and more Americans were alarmed by the German success and the *New York Times* stated that if Americans were true to their traditional ideals: 'We shall take our place in the line and play our part in the defence of freedom.'

The U.S.A. began to prepare for action. In 1940 Roosevelt called for £450 million to be spent on defence and in September of that year Congress approved legislation providing for compulsory military service. Roosevelt pointed out to the American people that if a neighbour's house was on fire one would lend him a garden hose without expecting him to pay for it. This approach led to the 'Lend-Lease' measures of March 1941. Under these measures the United States lent equipment to Britain for use during the duration of the war. Churchill called this 'the most unsordid act in history'.

Shortly after Hitler invaded Russia President Roosevelt went on a fishing trip. He left his yacht and boarded a cruiser out at sea and sped to Newfoundland for a special meeting with 'Former Naval Person', Winston Churchill's code name. The two leaders drew up the Atlantic Charter which was a statement of the ideals and aims of the two countries. The third article of the Charter stated that the nations signing respected 'the right of all peoples to choose the form of government under which they will live.' Nine exiled governments, Russia, and five other nations signed the Atlantic Charter which was a declaration of aims in general, not an alliance. Yet the United States was moving near to open war by this time. American warships were patrolling the western Atlantic and such actions as the sinking of the *Greer* by a U-Boat encouraged Roosevelt's hardening attitude against Germany. In November 1941 the United States extended lease-lend credit to Russia. Then the Japanese attack on Pearl Harbour led to Hitler and Mussolini declaring war on the United States on 11 December 1941. Germany and Italy faced Britain, Russia and the United States, and Japan faced Britain and the United States as 1942 dawned.

# *Battle of Stalingrad, 1942*
The Germans were on the defensive during the winter of 1941–
42. The Russians had lost much of their industrial area to the
Germans but they transferred factories and machinery east-
ward beyond the Urals. Production of war material was carried
on round the clock and the new 52-ton Russian tanks, 'white
mammoths', began to harass the Germans. As the spring weather came Hitler decided to concentrate his armies for a mighty
push in the south. He planned to drive deep into the Caucasus
to the oil fields and so cut the Russians off from their supply
while gaining more oil for his own armies. The Russians fought
fiercely but the Germans took Sevastopol and Rostov in July
1942. Then Hitler failed to keep up his concentrated pressure
and split his forces. One group struck towards the oil fields while
the other, under General Paulus, concentrated on Stalingrad.
The city was a large sprawling industrial centre on the Volga.
It was not only a symbol of the new industry of communist
Russia but it also controlled the oil supply route from the
Caspian to central Russia. On 22 August 1942 Hitler's attack
against Stalingrad began.

The city was reduced to rubble by a constant bombardment.
In this rubble and debris the German tanks became stuck and
the defenders of the city swarmed out of cellars and hiding
places to attack at close quarters with machine-guns, knives and
bayonets. The city became an open graveyard and the Germans
measured their advance in inches. As Marshal Zhukov said of
the Russians: 'Men died, but they did not retreat.' The German
attack ground to a halt. The generals asked Hitler to draw the
forces back from Stalingrad and regroup before winter closed
in again. Hitler refused to listen to them and so condemned
most of the Sixth Army under Paulus, about 330,000 men, to
die in Stalingrad. Hysterically Hitler shouted: 'Stay and fight!
I am not leaving the Volga!' The German Army had held the
line for the winter of 1941 and Hitler was determined that they
should not retreat in 1942, although the position was exposed
and impossible to supply.

The following account shows the grim resignation of the soldiers on the Russian front settling down for their second winter.

'Then one night the great freeze-up began, and winter was
with us, the second grim winter in that accursed country. Like

**IN THE PAGES OF HISTORY**

Low's cartoon comment on the Russian stand against the German attack

a black cloak the frost folded over the land. A supplies truck came round and brought us greatcoats, gloves, and caps with ear-flaps. Despite this issue, we froze miserably in our funkholes. In the morning we would be numb with cold, our rifles and guns completely coated with thick hoar-frost. As it left our mouths our breath was as dense as cigarette smoke and immediately solidified over the side-flaps of our caps its glittering crystals of ice. When shells came over, each detonation rang out with a new hard resonance and the clods of earth which were thrown high were like lumps of granite.

'Though apparently completely healed, last year's frost-bites on my heels began to be very painful again. I dared not let myself think of how long this cold would be with us, dared not remember everything would still be frozen up at the end of March.

'We just lay in our holes and froze, knowing that twenty-four hours later and forty-eight hours later we should be shivering precisely as we were now, and vainly longing to be relieved.

57

But there was no hope whatsoever, of relief, and that was the worst thing of all'.

In November 1942, as the weather grew cold, the Russians counter-attacked and cut off the head of the spear embedded in Stalingrad. The Sixth Army was cut off and Hitler refused

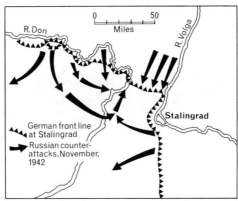

The Battle of Stalingrad

to allow them to try and break back to the German line. An attempt to relieve Paulus was beaten off in December 1942 and the Sixth Army was held in a closing ring. Hitler claimed that they held a fortress and made Paulus a field marshal. But General Zeitzler described the situation in clear terms: 'For the ordinary soldier fighting at Stalingrad, each day simply brought a renewed dose of hunger, need, privation, hardship of every sort, bitter cold, loneliness of soul, hopelessness. . . . It was a nightmare without end.'

This nightmare can be vividly seen in this letter which was one of the few to be flown out of the besieged Stalingrad.

'My hands are done for, and have been ever since the beginning of December. The little finger of my left hand is missing and—what's even worse—the three middle fingers of my right one are frozen. I can only hold my mug with my thumb and little finger. I'm pretty helpless; only when a man has lost any fingers does he see how much he needs them for the very smallest jobs. The best thing I can do with the little finger is shoot with it. My hands are finished. After all, even if I'm not fit for anything else, I can't go on shooting for the rest of my life. Or would I still make a gamekeeper, I wonder? That's a pretty grim kind of humour, I know. The only reason I write such things is to keep my nerves steady.

'A week ago Kurt Hahnke—you may remember him from the lectures we attended in '37—played the *Appassionata* on a grand piano in a little side street by the Red Square. Not a thing one sees every day of the week—a grand piano planted in the middle of a street. The house it came from had to be demolished, but I suppose they took pity on the piano and fetched it out beforehand. Every private soldier who passed that way had thumped around on it: Where else, I ask you, would you find pianos standing out in the street?'

By the end of January 1943 the famous Sixth Army, which had swept through Holland and Belgium in 1940, was worn out in Stalingrad. Paulus and his staff surrendered in a basement to a Russian lieutenant and the remains of the Sixth Army were taken prisoner. The Russians had suffered terrible losses in this battle. They lost more men at Stalingrad than the United States lost on all fronts during the entire war. Yet the defeat of the Sixth Army indicated that the ants could punish the elephant and that Hitler's hysterical 'no retreat' policy could destroy his fine armies.

# 7 Japanese Attack

## Some Important Dates, December 1941–December 1942

| | EUROPE | NORTH AFRICA | ASIA |
|---|---|---|---|
| *1941* | | | |
| December | German attack on Moscow halted. Italy and Germany declare war on U.S.A. | Tobruk relieved by Allied forces. | Japanese attack Pearl Harbour, sink *Prince of Wales* and *Repulse* and capture Hong Kong. |
| *1942* | | | |
| January | Russians hold out. | Rommel attacks in Libya. | Japanese invade Burma. |
| April | | | Fall of Bataan. |
| May | | | Battle of Coral Sea. |
| June | | Rommel held at El Alamein. | Battle of Midway Island. |
| August | Dieppe Raid. Germans attack Stalingrad. | Battle of El Alamein. | U.S. forces land in Solomons. |
| November | Germans occupy Vichy France. | Rommel retreats from Egypt. | Battle of the Solomon Islands |

## Pearl Harbour, December 1941

'Monica Conter, a young Army nurse, and Second Lieutenant Barney Benning of the Coast Artillery strolled out of the Pearl Harbour Officers' Club, down the path near the ironwood trees, and stood by the club landing, watching the launches take men back to the warships riding at anchor.

'They were engaged, and the setting was perfect. The workshops, the big hammerhead crane, all the paraphernalia of the Navy's great Hawaiian base were hidden by the night; the daytime clatter was gone; only the pretty things were left—

the moonlight . . . the dance music that drifted from the club
. . . the lights of the Pacific Fleet that shimmered across the
harbour.

'And there were more lights than ever before. For the first
weekend since July 4 all the battleships were in port at once.'[1]

All was peaceful at the American naval base on the evening
of 6 December 1941. Ninety-six ships of various sorts rode
quietly at anchor and just under 300 aircraft stood in neat rows
on the various airfields round Pearl Harbour. Only the aircraft
carriers were out on a routine cruise. Upon this peaceful scene
a Japanese force converged. Thirty-one ships including six carriers made up the main striking force while twenty-eight submarines, five carrying midget submarines, made up the advance
force. On 5 December 1941 this force had received the order,
'Climb Mount Niitake', which meant that they were to attack
Pearl Harbour swiftly and secretly.

At 6.45 a.m. on 7 December the American destroyer *Ward*
sank a midget submarine in the defensive sea area off Pearl
Harbour. Nobody dreamed that this submarine was part of a
planned attack. Shortly after seven the American radar began
to blip. A large force of planes was approaching. The Information Centre were unmoved as they were expecting twelve big
bombers from the mainland to add to their own squadrons.
The surprise was complete. On the *Nevada* the marine band
prepared to play the national anthem. Elsewhere, men ordered
poached eggs for breakfast, addressed Christmas presents,
glanced at the Sunday papers, played games, or just lay in their
bunks. On one of the landing stages two small boys threw their
fishing lines into the water and settled down to watch just another Sunday morning.

A few minutes before 8 a.m. this peaceful Sunday was blown
wide apart. Japanese planes swept in to the attack. American
sailors thought at first this must be a mock attack by their own
planes and they were stunned as torpedoes and bombs began
to burst and bullets sprayed around them. On the *Nevada* the
marine band finished playing *The Star-Spangled Banner* only
pausing an instant as bullets ripped into the deck around them.
Then they fled for cover and began to man the guns. Everywhere the Americans fought back desperately amidst terrible

[1] Walter Lord, *Day of Infamy*.

The battleship *California* settles slowly into the mud under the battering she received during the Japanese attack on Pearl Harbour

wreckage. A bomb went down the funnel of the *Arizona* and the battleship's magazine blew up. The ship became a raging inferno. The battleship *Oklahoma* was split open, heeled over, sank, and remained with her bottom sticking above the surface as further Japanese attacks came in. The Americans lost, with these two battleships, sixteen ships which were sunk or seriously damaged and 188 planes which were destroyed on the airfields. Over 100 more planes were damaged and 2,403 people were killed. Over half the people killed died when the *Arizona* blew up. The Japanese lost twenty-nine planes, one submarine, and all five midget submarines. At one blow they had crippled the U.S. Navy and gained control of the Pacific for their own purposes. The next day the United States declared war on Japan and President Roosevelt stated: 'We are going to win the war and we are going to win the peace that follows.'

## The Japanese Threat

Behind this sudden attack on Pearl Harbour lay years of mounting tension as Japan began to increase her influence in the Pacific and Asia. Japan had begun to build an empire in 1931 when Japanese troops invaded Manchuria in defiance of the League of Nations. In 1936 the Japanese government signed the Anti-Comintern Pact, an agreement to work against communism, with Germany and Italy. The following year Japan began military operations against the Chinese without a formal declaration of war. This struggle dragged on and the Japanese military leaders began to look for more spectacular conquests.

When World War Two began in 1939 the Japanese turned their attention to the rich sources of rice, coal, tin, rubber and oil in French Indo-China and the Dutch East Indies. They argued that they needed raw materials and they planned to build a 'Greater East Empire' in which the Japanese 'Sons of Heaven' would be the master race. World War Two seemed a good chance to put such plans into action and in September 1940 the Japanese made a general pact with Germany and Italy which would 'promote the prosperity of their peoples'.

The United States with her interests in the Pacific trade and the Philippine Islands watched Japanese expansion with suspicion. The U.S.A. objected to the Japanese use of American material in the war with China and began to place restrictions on trade with Japan in 1940. In July 1941 the Japanese government announced that they had assumed a protectorate over French Indo-China. Roosevelt then froze all Japanese credit in the U.S.A. and refused to export such things as machine tools and chemicals to Japan. Britain, China and the Dutch East Indies also refused to trade with Japan. The Japanese oil supply was cut by these restrictions and the war leaders demanded action before existing supplies ran short. Negotiations went on during the summer of 1941 and tension mounted. Churchill promised to support the United States and prepared to send naval forces to the Far East. The Japanese position hardened when the war minister, General Tojo, was made prime minister by the Emperor in October 1941. The Japanese decided to use armed force and surprise to smash United States Pacific power and win their empire.

## Japanese Success, 1941–42

The attack on Pearl Harbour was only one of a series of swift Japanese attacks. The American island bases of Guam and Wake Island fell in December 1941. Wake Island had the larger garrison and put up a heroic fight but the Japanese were too strong. The Allies were surprised at the speed and success of the Japanese attack. The Japanese were fit and well trained

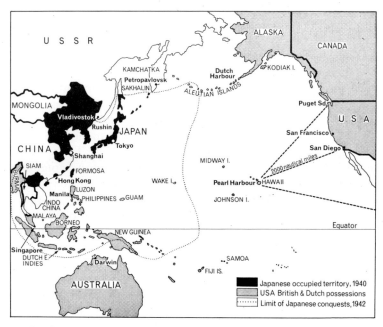

The Pacific war area

and they were skilled jungle fighters. Living on rations of hard rice they slipped through prepared positions and appeared in the rear to cause confusion. They also made full use of their powerful navy and air force.

Another blow was aimed at Malaya, Singapore, Hong Kong and Siam. Against this attack the British went into action in the south-western Pacific. The new battleship *Prince of Wales* and the cruiser *Repulse* had arrived in the Pacific as Churchill had promised. They now headed a force which intended to attack the Japanese transport ships before troops could be disembarked on the Malayan mainland. Admiral Phillips led his small force within range of Japanese bombers to carry out this attack. On 10 December 1941 Japanese planes struck and proved once more the importance of air power. Both the *Prince of Wales* and the *Repulse* were sunk and Admiral Phillips went down with his battleship. Churchill summed up the feeling of shock in Britain when he spoke to a grim House of Commons: 'In my whole experience I do not remember any naval blow so heavy or so painful as the sinking of the *Prince of Wales* and the *Repulse* on Monday last.' Hong Kong was bombed and Japanese soldiers landed at night and cut off the city's water supply. On Christmas Day 1941 the British garrison was forced to surrender. Singapore was considered to be the strongest naval base in the world. The British garrison there were confident that they could hold off any landing from the sea. They were not worried about attack down the northern peninsula for the area was covered with thick jungle and was very swampy. The Japanese landed in Malaya and their skilled jungle fighters pushed south towards Singapore's back door. The British forces fell back, unable to deal with such opponents. In January 1942 the causeway bridge from Singapore to the mainland peninsula was blown up and the garrison prepared to face a siege. Reinforcements arrived just in time to be taken by the Japanese who captured the reservoirs in February 1942 and so forced Singapore's garrison to surrender.

Yet another Japanese assault went in against the Americans in the Philippines. The Japanese were determined to take Manila, one of the finest natural harbours in the East. The day after the attack on Pearl Harbour the Japanese bombed the airfield near Manila in the Philippines and landed troops on the island of Luzon. On 2 January 1942 they took Manila and forced the Americans to withdraw to the Bataan Peninsula. This rugged area was protected from sea attack by the heavy guns on the island fortress of Corregidor and formed a magnificent defensive position. At Bataan the Americans fought grimly under General MacArthur. They were proud of their nickname, 'the battling bastards of Bataan', and they hung on as food ran short and they had to eat monkeys, snakes and any edible roots. Roosevelt ordered MacArthur to leave with his staff and set up headquarters in Australia. With his staff and family General MacArthur broke through enemy controlled territory and stated firmly: 'I came through and I shall return.' In April 1942 the Bataan garrison surrendered and were then forced to march for days goaded on by the bayonets of relentless Japanese guards. Many died on this death march and others died in the prison compounds. This action by the Japanese filled the American people with anger and they prepared to strike back. Yet the Japanese swept on. The island fortress of Corregidor held out until early May and then it too went down to the pounding attack.

Japan had won a ring of bases in these early months and her war leaders turned their eyes to Burma and to Australia. Through Burma ran the 800-mile Burma Road which had been used to supply the Chinese under Chiang Kai-shek in their battle with the Japanese. In January 1942 the Japanese launched their attack on Burma and by May most of the country was under their control. Supplies for the Chinese had to be sent by air over the 'Hump', the mountains of the Himalayas. During this advance the apparently invincible Japanese met with a surprising check. In 1937 Chiang Kai-shek had appointed an American, Chennault, to command the Chinese Air Force. In 1941 Chennault recruited volunteer pilots in America and his 'Flying Tigers' proved that Japanese planes could be defeated. The 'Flying Tigers' operated from Rangoon until it fell to the enemy. The seventy pilots flew an assortment of obsolete aircraft and destroyed at least 300 Japanese planes in the first few months of 1942.

The advance upon Australia went on at the same time as the Burma campaign. The Japanese intended to take Java to use as the key to their attack upon Australia and they landed small groups there in December 1941. The Allies tried to halt the main invasion with a combined fleet of five cruisers and nine destroyers. The Japanese wiped this fleet out in the Battle of the Java Sea, February 1942. By March all the Dutch East Indies were in Japanese hands.

The Americans were still stunned by the speed of this attack but they did manage to check the Japanese in an untidy battle in May 1942. American planes spotted a group of enemy ships in the Coral Sea and guided squadrons from carriers to the attack. The Japanese answered by sending in their carrier planes and the Battle of the Coral Sea was fought entirely by planes from carriers. Both sides withdrew after losses but the Japanese had been halted with heavy punishment. The American carrier *Lexington* was sunk along with one destroyer and a tanker while the Japanese lost one carrier, four cruisers and two destroyers. The Americans were beginning to come to grips with the enemy and were more determined than ever to strike back.

# 8 War at Sea: The Atlantic Battle

## Submarine Warfare

In 1939 Britain had over 21 million tons of merchant shipping sailing under her flag. This was over twice as much as any other single nation and almost twice as much as the thirteen and a half million tons owned by Japan, Germany and Italy combined. The densely populated island of Britain depended on supplies from overseas and so the merchant ships were vital to

National Savings Committee poster which shows the vital importance of Britain's merchant ships

her war effort. Hitler, on the other hand, was determined to gain his supplies from the lands of Europe and to make use of cleverly manufactured substitutes for such things as coffee and rubber. At the start of World War Two Britain declared a naval blockade of Germany. After December 1939 neutral ships were advised to get a 'navicert', a certificate from British officials overseas, to allow them to pass through the blockading patrols. This led to objections by neutral powers, especially the United States. They objected to British examination of neutral mail and questioned the right to blockade neutral ships. However, these irritations faded as the Germans launched a submarine 'sink at sight' policy in an attempt to cut British supplies. The first ship to be sunk was the passenger liner *Athenia*, which was torpedoed by a zealous U-Boat commander twelve hours after war had been declared.

The attack went on and was only restricted because the Germans had twenty-two ocean-going U-Boats at the outset. Under Admiral Doenitz, the German attacks increased and their submarine production developed rapidly. The danger to British supplies became serious and Churchill proclaimed early in 1941 that 'the battle of the Atlantic' was on. The quiet

A near miss by a German submarine during a convoy to Russia

heroes of this battle were the merchant seamen. Convoys of Allied ships crossed the Atlantic, struggled through Arctic seas, and steamed round the Cape of Good Hope. The members of the crews of these ships never knew when their ship might be destroyed by the sudden explosion of an enemy torpedo. They faced death in the cruel waters of the ocean or in the savage oil blaze of a stricken tanker so that Britain could survive. This was not a short glorious battle but a long grim struggle for survival.

### *Missing:* JOHN PUDNEY

Less said the better,
The bill unpaid, the dead letter,
No roses at the end
Of Smith, my friend.

Last words don't matter,
And there are none to flatter,
Words will not fill the post
Of Smith, the ghost.

For Smith, our brother,
Only son of loving mother,
The ocean lifted, stirred,
Leaving no word.

Success in this struggle swung to and fro. Escorted convoys, which the British used from the early days of the war, proved difficult targets for single submarines. The Germans then developed attacks by groups of submarines, wolf packs. These packs were called together when a lone U-Boat sighted a convoy. The submarines then shadowed the convoy on the surface by day for they knew from French sources that asdic—a system by which enemy submarines could be located by the echoes from sound waves—could not pick up surface raiders. At night the wolf pack would strike from all points of the compass with devastating effect. These packs refuelled from large 'mother' submarines which lay off the neutral Azores until Portugal allowed the Allies to use air bases there in October 1943. The Americans clashed with the U-Boats before they declared war. President Roosevelt issued his command to 'shoot on sight' any German ships when a U-Boat attacked the U.S.S. *Greer* in September 1941. When war was openly declared with the United States on 11 December 1941, the U-Boats closed in on the American coastal trade. Until convoys were used for this trade these ships proved easy targets as the Germans picked them off at night against the lighted line of the American coast. The Allies began to strike back after these heavy losses. The numbers of escort vessels were increased and systems of interlocking convoys were worked out by the United States Navy and the British Admiralty. Above all the Allies began to make full use of air power. Doenitz had boasted: 'Aircraft can no more eliminate the U-Boat than a crow can fight a mole.' This boast was proved to be unwise. Planes, like the four-engined Liberator, equipped with guns, miniature radar, and depth charges hunted U-Boats. The submarines had to surface to recharge batteries and to allow the crew a breath of fresh air and were destroyed when they were caught there by Allied planes. United States Army engineers built an airfield on the rugged Ascension Islands and with this base, halfway between Brazil and Africa, the Allies were able to seal the southern Atlantic off from German raiders. The 'crow' began to defeat the 'mole'.

In the last resort the Germans tried to build submarines that would not have to surface. The schnorkel (German slang for nose) tube was introduced to enable U-Boats to run their diesel engines under water, and new electric-driven submarines capable of high speeds and long periods under the surface were put on the production lines. Before these could be launched the Allies had invaded Europe and were sinking more submarines per month than they lost merchant ships.

A Sunderland puts a final burst of fire across a U-Boat's conning tower

*Phases of the Atlantic Submarine Struggle*

| | |
|---|---|
| September 1939 –March 1941 | Single U-Boats in action mainly in European waters. |
| April 1941 –November 1941 | U-Boat wolf packs move out into the Atlantic. |
| December 1941 –July 1942 | U-Boats very successful in American waters. 586 Allied ships sunk during these months. |
| August 1942 –May 1943 | Allied counter-attack begins. 43 U-Boats sunk in May 1943. |
| June 1943 –April 1945 | Counter-attack takes effect and U-Boat threat ends. |

## U-47 Attacks the British Fleet at Scapa Flow

On 8 October 1939 U-47 under the command of Captain Prien, slipped out of Kiel into the North Sea mists. The Germans had studied air photographs of the British fleet anchorage at Scapa Flow in the Orkneys. They noticed that the British had not yet blocked Kirk Sound, a narrow channel into the anchorage. Prien was to try and find his way through this channel on a moonless night in October.

The submarine scraped into Scapa Flow swinging perilously near the rocks in the whirling water of Kirk Sound. Prien was disappointed as he studied the ships at anchor. There were few targets but all seemed peaceful, so he took his time selecting two large targets. The first salvo of torpedoes hardly stirred the calm of the anchorage. Only one torpedo exploded against the cable of the battleship, *Royal Oak*, and the noise did not even disturb the crew below decks. Prien ordered his men to reload the tubes and fired a second salvo. This time the *Royal Oak* was struck and sunk. The British sailors were stunned and failed to spot the long shape of U-47 as it sailed out of the anchorage. A few days later Prien returned to Kiel and the German triumph warned Britain that the German sailors did not lack skill and daring. Prien went on to become one of the submarine aces of the German navy and was finally killed in 1940 when U-47 was sunk by a British destroyer.

## Surface Raiders

During the years between the world wars the Germans had

avoided the restrictions on building new battleships by launching three 'pocket battleships'. These were the size of cruisers but carried the guns of a battleship. Their weight was kept down by using welding instead of riveting and new lightweight guns. The *Graf Spee* was the last and finest of these ships and she was launched in 1934. At the start of World War Two Captain Langsdorff cruised the South Atlantic in the *Graf Spee* sinking at least nine ships. The Germans arranged for fuel to be taken from Brazil to the *Graf Spee*. The British waited for the pocket battleship to contact the fuel-laden freighters. On 13 December 1939 three British cruisers, *Exeter*, *Ajax* and *Achilles* opened fire upon the *Graf Spee*. After a running fight which lasted for fourteen hours the *Spee* retreated into neutral waters of the River Plate. The government of Uruguay refused to allow the ship to stay to refit. Outside the three cruisers kept watch and filled the air with radio messages as if a powerful fleet supported them. Captain Langsdorff took his ship along the river on 17 December and people thronged the shore to watch the expected sea battle. The battle never came. The *Graf Spee* stopped and was blown up by the captain and crew who escaped in the boats. Captain Langsdorff shot himself three days later. He had scuttled his ship upon orders from Hitler and, bitter at the disgrace, he wrapped himself in the flag of the old Imperial German Navy, rejecting the swastika, before he killed himself.

The next threat from a German surface raider came in 1941 when the German battleship *Bismarck* with her eight 15-inch guns sailed into the Atlantic with the cruiser *Prinz Eugen*. The

The *Graf Spee* in flames off Montevideo

The *Bismarck* in action against H.M.S. *Hood*

threat from such ships meant that each Atlantic convoy had
to be escorted by a battleship and now the threat was shown
to be serious. The British home fleet closed round the raiders
which damaged the battleship *Prince of Wales* and sank the
battlecruiser *Hood* on the first contact. A war correspondent
described the engagement.

'The end of the mighty *Hood* was an almost unbelievable
nightmare. Shortly after the engagement began shells hit the
twenty-one-year-old battle-cruiser. There was a bright sheet of
flame and she blew up, apparently blasted by an unlucky hit
in her thinly armoured magazine loaded with powder. Parts
of her hull were thrown hundreds of feet into the air and in a
few minutes all that remained was a patch of smoke on the
water and some small bits of wreckage.'

Britain was stunned by this loss and to make matters worse
the German ships gave the pursuing force the slip. The only
trace of the *Bismarck* was a patch of oil from her damaged supply
system. After thirty-one hours aircraft from the *Ark Royal* spotted the fleeing *Bismarck* in the Atlantic. On 26 March 1941
planes from the British carrier torpedoed the *Bismarck*, which
was finally finished off by a merciless pounding from British
ships. The importance of air power had been underlined by
this action.

Hitler decided to move his surface ships to Norway. He rea-
lised that the Atlantic was not a safe hunting ground and he
feared a British landing in Norway. Furthermore the ships in
Norwegian harbours would threaten the Allied convoy route

73

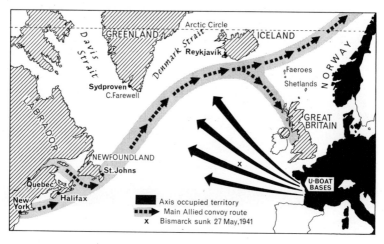

Axis occupied territory
Main Allied convoy route
x   Bismarck sunk 27 May, 1941

The Battle of the Atlantic

supplying aid to Russia. In February 1942 the *Scharnhorst*, *Gneisenau* and *Prinz Eugen* moved out of Brest and raced up the Channel. This daring move was entirely successful and the ships easily dodged the attack by Swordfish torpedo planes which was all the surprised Admiralty could use against the Germans. In Norway these ships, with the battleship *Tirpitz*, formed a dangerous threat to the convoys to Russia. The convoy that sailed for Russia in June 1942 was attacked by six U-Boats and then by the *Tirpitz*. The ships scattered and twenty-two out of thirty-three were lost.

At length, on Boxing Day 1943, the *Scharnhorst* was caught by a squadron of British cruisers and the battleship *Duke of York*. After a brisk fight the *Scharnhorst* was sunk. Before this success in the open sea the British had struck back at the *Tirpitz*. The weapon used was the midget submarine. Forty-eight feet long, these craft carried a crew of four, one of whom was a diver who swam out from the tiny submarine to cut through torpedo nets. The submarine carried four tons of delayed action explosive to lay under the hull of the target ship. Two of these submarines, X6 and X7, out of a group of six towed over to Norway by conventional submarines, reached the *Tirpitz*. X6, under the command of Lieutenant Cameron, followed a picket boat through the torpedo nets and released her explosive just as she was spotted and came under fire. The crew were picked up and taken on board the *Tirpitz* where they waited, knowing that their charges were due to go off at any moment. X7, under the command of Lieutenant Place, also managed to wriggle through the torpedo nets and lay charges. Shortly after eight on the morning of 24 September 1943 the *Tirpitz* was lifted five or six feet upwards by an underwater explosion. Chaos reigned on board the great ship and when X7 was spotted every available gun opened fire. Place decided to abandon the submarine but two of his crew were overcome by poisonous fumes and only he and his diver survived. The Germans took six months to repair the *Tirpitz* and then the British attacked again. Barracuda bombers from aircraft carriers and a base at Archangel hit the German battleship fifteen times. Finally, another force of bombers put the *Tirpitz* completely out of action in November 1944. The menace of surface raiders was at an end after five years of war in the Atlantic.

## An Unusual Weapon

During September and October 1939 twelve merchant ships were mysteriously sunk as they entered British ports through channels which had just been swept clear of mines. In November Hitler hinted that Germany had a new secret weapon and British concern increased when six more ships were sunk on their way into the Thames.

Then on 22 November 1939 observers on the coast saw a German plane drop some large object attached to a parachute into the tidal mud near Shoeburyness in Essex. The next day this object was located and inspected before the tide came in and covered it. Early in the afternoon a small party from the naval mine department began to dismantle this strange weapon as the sea washed back. They worked swiftly to remove the detonators, risking the danger of an explosion from a false move. By evening the mine had been removed and taken to Portsmouth for further study. These mines detonated when the magnetic field of a passing ship completed an electrical circuit. The answer to these magnetic mines was then worked out. British ships had to be demagnetised by passing an electric cable round the hull. This system, termed 'degaussing',[1] was used at once and Hitler's secret weapon in the sea became harmless.

[1] Named after the German scientist Gauss (1777–1855) who devised the principle of magnetic flux.

# 9 Air and Sea War in the Pacific

*' It is only by shipping that the United States or indeed we ourselves can intervene in the eastern or the western theatre.'*

Winston Churchill, 1942

## Some Important Dates, August 1942–October, 1944

| | EUROPE | N. AFRICA & ITALY | ASIA |
|---|---|---|---|
| **1942** | | | |
| August | Germans attack Stalingrad. | Battle of El Alamein. | U.S. forces land on Guadalcanal. |
| November | German forces take over Vichy | Rommel retreats from Egypt. | Naval battle in Solomon Islands |
| **1943** | | | |
| February | Germans surrender Stalingrad. | | |
| March | | Montgomery attacks Mareth line. | Battle of Bismarck Sea. |
| July | | Allies invade Sicily. | U.S. and Australian forces advance in New Guinea. |
| September | Russians retake Smolensk. | Allied landings in Italy. | |
| **1944** | | | |
| June | Allied landings in France. | Rome taken by Allies. | Japanese retreat in Burma. |
| October | Metz falls to Allies. | Warsaw rising crushed by Germans. | Battle of Leyte. |

Control of the Atlantic was vital to Britain's survival in the fight against Germany. In the struggle with Japan the Americans and their allies learnt that control of the Pacific was the key to success. A glance at the map (page 64) shows that the area of the Japanese advance was mainly sea. Soldiers and supplies had to be carried in ships or dropped from planes and heavy equipment had to be landed from ships. The Americans produced an entire new range of landing craft when they counter-attacked in the Pacific. Eighty thousand landing craft were built, ranging from the LCR (landing craft, rubber), which held six men, to the LCT (landing craft, tank). Such craft were easy victims for warships and planes and so the Pacific struggle was dominated by the fight for control of the sea and the air. In addition the control of the air largely depended on aircraft carriers because there were few air-strips in the area of the Pacific. The Americans under James Doolittle actually launched a bombing raid upon Tokyo from a carrier on 18 April 1942.

In May 1942 the Japanese advance received a check at the Battle of the Coral Sea which was fought between American and Japanese carrier planes. This check and the daring raid on Tokyo provoked a Japanese attack upon Midway Island. The attacking force was made up of two hundred ships including eleven battleships and eight carriers. The Japanese relied on surprise to help this powerful force take Midway Island. Unfortunately for them, the Americans had broken the main Japanese code and so were able to prepare for this attack. Three

U.S. landing craft manœuvre off a Pacific island

carriers and seven heavy cruisers were carefully deployed and the Americans went in against the carriers which had launched their planes against the airstrip on Midway Island. The Japanese pilots returned from their raid only to find their mother ships under savage attack. The Japanese lost four carriers and a heavy cruiser and broke off the action before their surface ships were fully engaged. The Americans had halted the Japanese at a cost. They lost one carrier, a destroyer and 147 aircraft in this air and sea battle. The Japanese had become too confident and had launched this long distance sea attack expecting another Pearl Harbour. The Americans had shown that they could strike back hard and successfully against their powerful enemy and make full use of the new skills of carrier warfare.

## Guadalcanal

On 7 August 1942 the Americans landed two Marine divisions on Guadalcanal and its surrounding small islands in the Solomon Islands. This action underlined the vital importance of the control of the sea in the Pacific battle. A series of naval battles were fought round the Solomon Islands while the Marines hacked their way through the jungle swamps of Guadalcanal and learnt the tricks of Japanese jungle warfare from hard experience. In one action the Australian cruiser, *Canberra*, was sunk while guarding the beaches. In others the Americans tried to intercept the *Tokyo Express*, the Japanese forces bringing reinforcements from their bases in other Solomon Islands. The fifth and fiercest battle of the Solomon Islands was fought on the night of 13 November 1942. The Japanese fleet took a pounding from a much smaller American force during this battle. The Americans rushed in to close quarters and found that they were safe from the Japanese heavy guns which could not be depressed enough to fire at short ranges. The Japanese lost two battleships, one cruiser, three destroyers and ten troop transports and failed to send in support to their men on Guadalcanal. By February 1943 the Japanese had to withdraw from Guadalcanal and the American advance began. During this advance success depended on the ability to deal with the reinforcements sent in by sea and to move troops easily. On 1 March 1943 American airmen spotted a fleet of twenty-two Japanese ships sailing to reinforce New Guinea against Allied advance. This fleet was attacked and virtually destroyed by American planes in the Battle of the Bismarck Sea. The Allies were able to advance nearly 3,000 miles because they co-ordinated air, sea and land forces and struck at the Japanese supply lines across the sea.

## *The Battle of Leyte, October 1944*

The American advance continued and in July 1944 General Douglas MacArthur flew from the Pacific battleground to Pearl Harbour. There he met President Roosevelt who asked him: 'Douglas, where do we go from here?' MacArthur replied: 'Leyte, Mr President; and then Luzon.' The Americans were heading back to the Philippines. The landings took place on Leyte, in the centre of the Philippine Islands, in October 1944, and MacArthur said: 'People of the Philippines, I have returned.' In this way he reminded people of the promise he made in 1942. The question remained as to whether MacArthur and his force could stay in the Philippines. The Japanese remembered their success against the Americans cut off at Bataan in 1942 and they decided to destroy this new landing by smashing its naval support and the landing craft which kept it going. They threw into this attack most of their fleet. Three groups set out against the Americans in the Philippines. The Japanese planned to lure the fleet defending the beaches at Leyte away and then slip in and destroy the amphibious craft which formed MacArthur's lifeline. In part their plan worked, for a section

U.S. marines move up through the jungle against Japanese positions

of the American fleet rushed north to deal with the enemy carrier force there, leaving the northern approach to the Leyte Gulf unprotected. While the Japanese fleet in the south was smashed their central force fought its way through to the unguarded approach to the Leyte beachhead. This situation resulted in the great cry on 25 October 1944 of: 'Enemy battle-fleet in sight.'

Seven destroyers and six light carriers lay off the beachhead when an American patrol plane sent in the report of the enemy fleet approaching. The commander of this force could hardly believe the news. Then the sea round his ships began to spout coloured fountains as the first salvos struck. The Japanese put different coloured dye in their shells to mark the shots from various ships. One American sailor was heard to comment: 'Hell! They're shooting at us in Technicolor.' The small American force went into action to save the landing craft and their force in the Philippines. The destroyers rushed in to attack. The *Johnston* was nearest to the enemy fleet and although she was severely hit she managed to set fire to a Japanese cruiser. The other destroyers also went in with their torpedoes so that the light carriers had time to send up their planes. This gallant destroyer force held the Japanese attack until American planes began to attack. The Japanese destroyer captain who finally sank the *Johnston* stood at the salute as she went down. Only about half the crew of this destroyer were picked up from the shark infested water and one man could show the marks where a shark had gripped him twice and then let him go. The Japanese fleet commander did not spend time in saluting the Americans when he saw the carrier planes swooping to the attack. He had no wish to lose his powerful ships to air attack and so he ordered a withdrawal just as his fleet found the range of the carrier group. They only had time to sink one American carrier and damage two others before the range grew too great again. The gallant destroyer attack had saved MacArthur's lifeline and the complete action had cost the Japanese thirty-three warships including four carriers and three battleships. After this battle the Japanese were not able to threaten American landings seriously and as an immediate result Japanese troops in the Philippines were cut off. The Americans were winning control of the Pacific.

## ' *Divine Wind* '

The Japanese have a legend that a divine wind, 'Kamikaze' was sent by the Sun Goddess to wreck the fleet of Kublai Khan in 1281. In 1944 the Japanese leaders decided that they would have to arrange their own 'Kamikaze' to destroy the American fleet. Japanese pilots were ready to die for their country and they cheerfully drank a toast to the Emperor before locking themselves in a suicide plane. These were of two types. The 'Oka' (Cherry Blossom), was a piloted bomb of which only a few were made in 1945. Most 'Kamikaze' attacks were made

A captured Japanese suicide plane

in planes which had been stripped down and then loaded with explosive set to go off on contact. These deadly planes attacked American ships in swarms and aimed especially at the vulnerable aircraft carriers. Some Japanese planes were sent to draw off the defenders while the 'Kamikaze' waited for a chance to dive down to death on an enemy ship. These attacks sunk thirty-four American ships and damaged a further 288 but they did not halt the Allied advance. The fantastic bravery of the 'Kamikaze' pilots was not sufficient to defeat the strength and technical skill of the United States.

# 10 Air Attack

*' Then there will be nothing left but a heap of ruins.'*
(*I was a Nazi Flier*, Leske, 1941)

## The Germans Bomb Britain, 1940–41

German pilots like Leske took part in the Battle of Britain and
towards the end of this battle Hitler decided to switch the
'Luftwaffe' to bombing raids on cities. The Germans were not
really prepared for such a switch and their leaders were not
entirely clear as to what they hoped to gain by these raids.
Hitler hoped that Britain would be forced to surrender quickly
and that the German people would enjoy revenge for the bombing of their cities. On 25 August 1940 the British began the
night-bombing of German towns as part of their attack against
the power of Germany. The day before a German pilot had
dropped his bombs on London against orders. Out of this confusion came the air attack on Britain which was popularly
called the 'Blitz'. The German 'Luftwaffe' had been built to

King George VI and Queen Elizabeth visit parts of London battered during the
'Blitz'

Civil Defence workers listen and dig for victims trapped beneath rubble. An N.F.S. trailer pump stands by in case of fire

operate with the German armed forces and they did not have many long range bombers. However, the 'Blitz' battered British cities and when incendiary bombs were used burnt large areas.

From 7 September until 2 November 1940 London was bombed every night. Under this bombardment from the air the spirit of the people remained high. The air-raid services were filled by voluntary recruits and local fire brigades were re-organised as the N.F.S., National Fire Service. Everybody learnt how to handle stirrup-pumps and how to manage business when normal transport became upset. Bombs landed on London Zoo and the papers reported that 'the morale of the monkeys remained unaffected'. The House of Commons building was destroyed and the Commons had to move into the House of Lords. Buckingham Palace was damaged but King George VI was often on the scene soon after a severe raid to cheer and encourage people as they struggled to save those trapped under debris. Most Londoners slept at home even during the worst raids but a large number slept in the underground stations or in their own Anderson shelters. These were built on designs sent out by Anderson, the home secretary at the time. J. B. Priestley, the author, has described the sparkling spirit aroused by the 'Blitz' when he was broadcasting from

83

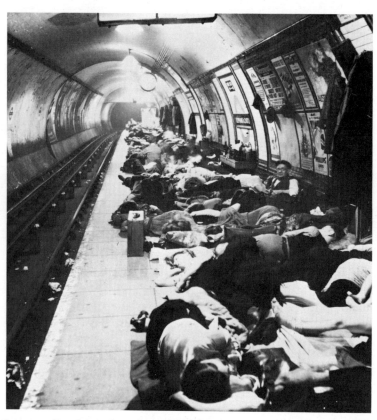
Large numbers slept in the underground stations

London in 1940. Priestley was about to enjoy a night in a shelter bedroom after his hotel had been hit by a bomb and he slowly prepared for a comfortable night disregarding the remote sounds from the mad world above. But it was a night of incendiaries: 'I was about to enjoy those clean sheets when I had to jump into my clothes again. The house was on fire.

'The bright eyes of danger have never fascinated me. If I am not quite a coward, I am much closer to being one than I am to being any sort of hero. Yet I can honestly declare that on the whole I enjoyed that time, those splintered nights, those mornings when the air was the freshest ever tasted.'[1]

The danger from German bombs brought people together.

[1] J. B. Priestley, *Margin Released*.

Number 23 Queen Victoria Street collapses after being hit during an air-raid

All were united against the enemy and, like Priestley, found enjoyment in merely being alive. Bombing did not destroy the spirit of the people; it encouraged it to burn brightly.

The German bombing raids continued until well into 1941, when most of the 'Luftwaffe' was needed on the Russian front. London was not the only city to suffer as the Germans also attacked provincial centres. Hull, Plymouth, Bristol, Liverpool, Manchester and Birmingham were all heavily bombed but perhaps the most famous of these attacks was the raid on Coventry. Coventry was attacked on the night of 14 November 1940 and much of the city including the cathedral was destroyed. Yet, in spite of this savage raid, the factories in Coventry were back in full production within five days. The raids did not halt production and did not break the morale of the people. It is difficult to assess the damage that they did do. Thirty thousand people were killed in the raids and a great number of houses and buildings were destroyed. At the same time people suffered from the stresses brought about by lack of sleep and nervous strain. Civilians were in the line of battle in a very real sense in World War Two.

YOUR COURAGE
YOUR CHEERFULNESS
YOUR RESOLUTION

WILL BRING
US VICTORY

A poster showing the way in which everybody was involved in the war

## Germany Suffers from Bombing

German air power had proved most effective when it was used as part of the 'Blitzkrieg' tactics. The bombing of Britain had not proved a success and it is perhaps surprising that the Allies should have put so much effort and skill into their bombing raids on Germany. The desire to hit back and the belief that German industrial production could be crippled led to the bombing offensive against Germany. On 30 May 1942 the R.A.F. made the first thousand bomber raid on Cologne. The Germans bombed towns like Exeter in reply to such raids. The spirit of the German people was not broken by air attacks nor was German production halted. In June 1944, in spite of the massive air raids, Germany was better stocked with munitions than at any time in the war.

Sir Arthur Harris, commander-in-chief of Bomber Command in 1942, was convinced that bombing would bring Germany to her knees. In 1943 the American Flying Fortresses made a series of daylight raids against precise targets. The German fighters proved that this was an expensive policy and the British continued to bomb area targets at night. Bomber Command did carry out a famous raid at night on a precise target in 1943. Two of the Ruhr dams were broken by special 'bouncing bombs' but the damage from the flood water was less than expected because the third dam held. The bombing

A British bomber drops its bombs on German positions in North Italy

raids continued and the centres of cities like Hamburg, Essen and Berlin were reduced to a 'heap of ruins'. The raids were expensive and in 1944 British Bomber Command was placed under Eisenhower in preparation for D-Day and the invasion of France.

Again it is difficult to assess the result of the bombing attacks on Germany. Since the end of the war it has become clear that German production was not halted by the bombing at the time. The real legacy of the air attacks was the ruined cities which had

Armourers sweep away the snow from 500 lb bombs waiting to be loaded on to R.A.F. bombers

to be restored after the fighting was over. The cost of these raids was heavy. The British lost 22,000 planes and over 79,000 airmen while the Americans lost 18,000 planes and almost the same number of airmen as the British.

## The Airmen

Behind these losses and the thousands of tons of bombs dropped during the war stand the figures of the men who flew the bombers and of those who kept the planes flying. Pilots, air crews and ground crews worked round the clock to keep up the pressure on Germany. The air war bred a special spirit of its own. A spirit which sprang from the nearness of death on missions.

*For Johnny:* JOHN PUDNEY

Do not despair
For Johnny-head-in-air;
He sleeps as sound
As Johnny underground.

Fetch out no shroud
For Johnny-in-the-cloud;
And keep your tears
For him in after years.

Better by far
For Johnny-the-bright-star,
To keep your head,
And see his children fed.

88

Ground crews had the unglamorous task of sending the bombers off into the dusk and then waiting sadly for the shattered return flight at dawn. During the night the crew of the bomber were very much on their own and many acts of bravery took place in planes miles above the earth and miles away from home. In October 1945 Sergeant Norman Jackson received the Victoria Cross for an 'almost incredible feat' which he had performed over a year before.

On 26 April 1944 Sergeant Jackson prepared to fly on the last operation of his second tour with Bomber Command. In the morning he heard that his wife had given birth to a son and he felt happy and excited as he boarded a Lancaster bomber as the flight engineer.

The Lancaster dropped its bombs and started upon the return journey flying four miles above Germany. An enemy fighter suddenly attacked and Jackson was wounded by cannon-shells as the big bomber swung to and fro to dodge the attack. Suddenly fire broke out on one wing of the bomber. Jackson asked the pilot for permission to try to put out the fire. The pilot agreed to allow Jackson to do what he could and the sergeant climbed out into the night as the bomber roared on at two hundred miles an hour. His parachute opened and spilled into the cockpit where the rest of the bomber crew collected it up and paid out the cords. Jackson worked his way along the wing. Then he slipped and just managed to hang on to the edge of the wing as the fire extinguisher he was carrying was swept away into the darkness.

The fire began to spread and soon covered Jackson as he hung on desperately. Eventually he was forced to let go of the wing and he fell away from the blazing bomber with his burning parachute trailing behind him. Four members of the crew managed to escape from the burning Lancaster which was soon out of control and crashed. Jackson broke an ankle as he landed heavily on German soil. Badly burned and wounded he managed to crawl to a cottage and was made prisoner. A year later he returned to Britain and received reward for his act of heroism in the night skies above Germany.

## Hitler's Wonder Weapons

As the war went on there was increasing talk of Hitler's

A flying bomb crashing down on central London

'Wunderwaffen' or wonder weapons which would win the war for Germany. In 1943 Allied commandos had destroyed the German heavy-water installation in Norway and so upset the German researches into atomic weapons. During the same year the R.A.F. bombed Peenemünde on the Baltic, for air photographs showed rocket launching bases there. Further attacks went in on the launching sites on the French coast between Calais and Cherbourg. Seven days after the Allied landings in Normandy, Hitler's rockets were launched against targets in Britain. They were aimed at London and only about a quarter of the 8,000 fired from 13 to 20 June 1944 reached their target through the heavy coastal defences. These V1 rockets were Hitler's 'vergeltungswaffen' or vengeance weapon and were termed 'doodlebugs' by the British people. They were a small pilotless jet-propelled plane which carried one ton of explosive at more than 300 miles an hour on a predetermined course. The V2 rocket was first fired in early August 1944. This rocket carried a ton of explosive at supersonic speed and was almost impossible to intercept and destroy before it hit a target. Fortunately for the people of London this new air attack did not last long because the main launching sites were captured by the Allied armies late in August 1944. Over 8,000 people lost their lives from Hitler's wonder weapons and they proved that Germany was far from destroyed in 1944.

# 11 People at War

*'In spite of everything I believe that people are really good at heart.'*
*The Diary of Anne Frank*

## Life Under Hitler

Anne Frank spent two years of her short life hiding from the Nazis in Amsterdam. In August 1944 her family's secret hiding place was discovered and, aged fifteen, she was taken away to a concentration camp because she was Jewish. She died in the camp but her diary was found in 1947 and has been translated into more than twenty languages. Her faith in humanity and her courage symbolise the opposition to Hitler's rule over Europe.

By 1942 the Germans had conquered most of Europe. The conquered lands were plundered in the interests of Hitler's master race. Areas such as Austria and the Sudetenland were united with Germany. Other areas were placed under commissioners who ruled according to the race and behaviour of the population in their area. Denmark was allowed to retain her own monarch and parliament because she was a Nordic country. In Czechoslovakia the Slav inhabitants were treated savagely by Heydrich, the Nazi Protector of the area. A group of Czech patriots tried to kill Heydrich in May 1942. He died of his wounds and the Nazis decided on a terrible revenge. They were convinced that the village of Lidice had given shelter to the group of patriots so they wiped out the entire village. Every male adult was shot, the women and children dispersed, the buildings pulled down, and the name of the village erased from all maps. Throughout occupied Europe the Gestapo, the Nazi secret police, worked with such ruthlessness. At any time black-shirted raiding parties might appear to round up people for the labour camps in Germany.

The people who suffered most cruelly from this grim rule were the Jews. Hitler regarded the Jewish people with hysterical hatred and turned the full force of a modern police state on

me Circle Library
BUSINESS AS USUAL
— AT —
Id Gate House
AND THE BRIDGE,
ST. SAMPSON'S

# Evening Press

GUERNSEY, MONDAY, JULY 1, 1940    GRATIS

# ORDERS OF THE COMMANDANT OF THE GERMAN FORCES IN OCCUPATION OF THE ISLAND OF GUERNSEY

(1)—ALL INHABITANTS MUST BE INDOORS BY 11 P.M. AND MUST NOT LEAVE THEIR HOMES BEFORE 6 A.M.

(2)—WE WILL RESPECT THE POPULATION IN GUERNSEY; BUT, SHOULD ANYONE ATTEMPT TO CAUSE THE LEAST TROUBLE, SERIOUS MEASURES WILL BE TAKEN AND THE TOWN WILL BE BOMBED.

(3)—ALL ORDERS GIVEN BY THE MILITARY AUTHORITY ARE TO BE STRICTLY OBEYED.

(4)—ALL SPIRITS MUST BE LOCKED UP IMMEDIATELY, AND NO SPIRITS MAY BE SUPPLIED, OBTAINED OR CONSUMED HENCEFORTH. THIS PROHIBITION DOES NOT APPLY TO STOCKS IN PRIVATE HOUSES.

(5)—NO PERSON SHALL ENTER THE AERODROME AT LA VILLIAZE.

(6)—ALL RIFLES, AIRGUNS, PISTOLS, REVOLVERS, DAGGERS, SPORTING GUNS, AND ALL OTHER WEAPONS WHATSOEVER, EXCEPT SOUVENIRS, MUST, TOGETHER WITH ALL AMMUNITION, BE DELIVERED AT THE ROYAL HOTEL BY 12 NOON TO-DAY, JULY 1.

(7)—ALL BRITISH SAILORS, AIRMEN AND SOLDIERS ON LEAVE IN THIS ISLAND MUST REPORT AT THE POLICE STATION AT 9 A.M. TO-DAY, AND MUST THEN REPORT AT THE ROYAL HOTEL.

(8)—NO BOAT OR VESSEL OF ANY DESCRIPTION, INCLUDING ANY FISHING BOAT, SHALL LEAVE THE HARBOURS OR ANY OTHER PLACE WHERE THE SAME IS MOORED, WITHOUT AN ORDER FROM THE MILITARY AUTHORITY, TO BE OBTAINED AT THE ROYAL HOTEL. ALL BOATS ARRIVING FROM JERSEY, FROM SARK OR FROM HERM, OR ELSEWHERE, MUST REMAIN IN HARBOUR UNTIL PERMITTED BY THE MILITARY TO LEAVE.

THE CREWS WILL REMAIN ON BOARD. THE MASTER WILL REPORT TO THE HARBOURMASTER, ST. PETER-PORT, AND WILL OBEY HIS INSTRUCTIONS.

(9)—THE SALE OF MOTOR SPIRIT IS PROHIBITED, EXCEPT FOR USE ON ESSENTIAL SERVICES, SUCH AS DOCTORS' VEHICLES, THE DELIVERY OF FOODSTUFFS, AND SANITARY SERVICES WHERE SUCH VEHICLES ARE IN POSSESSION OF A PERMIT FROM THE MILITARY AUTHORITY TO OBTAIN SUPPLIES.

THESE VEHICLES MUST BE BROUGHT TO THE ROYAL HOTEL BY 12 NOON TO-DAY TO RECEIVE THE NECESSARY PERMISSION.

THE USE OF CARS FOR PRIVATE PURPOSES IS FORBIDDEN.

(10)—THE BLACK-OUT REGULATIONS ALREADY IN FORCE MUST BE OBSERVED AS BEFORE.

(11)—BANKS AND SHOPS WILL BE OPEN AS USUAL.

(Signed) THE GERMAN COMMANDANT OF THE ISLAND OF GUERNSEY

JULY 1, 1940.

The front page of the Guernsey Paper carrying the German commandant's orders, 1 July 1940

**IN OCCUPIED TERRITORY**

Low's cartoon comments on the German occupation of Europe. Hitler and Himmler discuss the situation

them. Over five and a half million Jews disappeared under the rule of the German Nazis. More than 400,000 died in the Warsaw area alone. The terrible death camps such as Buchenwald, Dachau, Auschwitz and Belsen were discovered by the advancing Allied armies in 1945. The full horror of a policy of mass extermination became known to the world. The Nazis in these camps had systematically killed thousands of innocent people. Many died in gas chambers which had been disguised as showers, while others were used as human guinea pigs for experiments. Others died from hunger, torture and disease in the miserable compounds of the camps.

Hitler had claimed in his book, *Mein Kampf*, that the greatest spirit could be broken by the use of a rubber truncheon. His rule over Europe was obviously based on such thinking. Furthermore the conquered peoples were regarded as slaves who should work for their German superiors. The Russians evacuated many people from Kharkov in the Ukraine as the Germans advanced in October 1941. Seven hundred thousand people were left and when the Russians returned after a year

93

and a half in February 1943 only half that number still lived in Kharkov. One hundred and twenty thousand young people had been taken to Germany for slave labour, nearly 80,000 had died from hunger and 30,000, many of them Jews, had been killed by the Germans. Another large group of over 100,000 had fled from the city into the surrounding villages where they were safer from the Germans. Public hangings, open Black Market dealing, the removal of young people to Germany for slave labour, starvation rations and a general reign of terror marked the German occupation of Soviet territory and left a legacy of hatred. The children in Kharkov used to chant a verse about the bread ration to annoy the German soldiers. The song ended:

> 'To hell with Hitler's 300 grammes;
> Let's have workers' clubs and cinemas,
> And Stalin's kilograms.'

Some people in the occupied areas were prepared to co-operate with their German rulers. Mussert, leader of the Dutch Fascists, worked with the occupation forces in Holland as did Quisling in Norway. Mussert and Quisling were both tried and executed by their countrymen after the war was over. In Vichy France Pétain set up a form of police state and co-operated with the Nazis who planned to turn France into an agricultural storehouse for Germany. Yet many people refused to accept Hitler's rule and refused to bow beneath the rubber truncheon. The resistance movements became more and more effective as the war went on. Armed bands sniped at German soldiers and blew up bridges while factory workers turned out dud shells for the German army. Thousands of Germans were attacked at night in Holland and their dead bodies were dumped in the canals. The 'Maquis' in France, the 'Chetniks' in Yugoslavia, the 'Andartes' in Greece, formed resistance armies which constantly harried the occupation forces. Secret routes were worked out for Allied airmen and escaped prisoners while underground newspapers, like the Belgian 'Free Belgium', flourished. Danes who joined their underground resistance called themselves 'moles' and all over Europe the struggle against Hitler's powerful forces went on. In Moscow a pocket book called *The Partisan's Guide* sold thousands of copies during 1942. The B.B.C. broadcast information to the people of Europe and saboteurs

A nineteen-year-old French girl who fought against the Germans in the French resistance

trained in Britain were dropped in occupied areas to link up with the local patriots in their struggle for survival. Hitler's new order for Europe was never accepted in the occupied countries.

## Propaganda

During World War Two both sides used propaganda to persuade people that they were right and that they would win. 'The Germans are a super-race destined to rule the world!' was a typical slogan produced by Goebbels who was in charge of German propaganda. Everything was used in the battle for minds and the Germans even discussed distributing propaganda leaflets by attaching them to the legs of migrating storks. William Joyce, an Anglo-American Fascist who had become a naturalised German, broadcast from Germany and earned the title 'Lord Haw Haw'. Stories and rumours spread easily under war conditions and people often suffered from such tales after the war had ended. P. G. Wodehouse was unfairly condemned

95

for giving a light-hearted radio talk to the Germans about life in an internment camp after his capture by the Germans in France.

Two sides of the same story

In fact neither side believed much of the propaganda produced by the other, though there were one or two notable successes. The Germans dropped a large number of leaflets over France before they overran the country. These were in the shape of green leaves and carried the words: 'If you fight England's battles, your soldiers will fall like autumn leaves.' These words struck home as did the war reports in the accurate Allied paper for German troops, *Frontpost*. The Allies were also successful with their safe conduct passes which encouraged thousands of German and Italian troops to surrender. Most Japanese propaganda was crude and clumsy. A woman broadcaster, Tokyo Rose, gave a regular record programme of propaganda talks given in silky tones. These broadcasts were regarded as a huge joke by Allied soldiers.

Many of the Allies remembered the ugly atrocity stories which had been used in World War One and they were determined not to listen to such stories again. Newspapers such as the *Daily Mirror* achieved a huge circulation and the ordinary Briton looked for information in the paper. The government set up a Ministry of Information in 1939 for dealing with propaganda but the *Daily Mirror* was often critical of the government's policy and in 1942 Churchill wanted to suppress the paper for its outspoken statements. The German press was carefully censored by Goebbels who only allowed losses to be known when he wanted the Germans to make a greater effort to protect their country. This situation meant that the Germans firmly believed that they were fighting for a new European empire while the Allies saw Nazi rule as an evil which had to be destroyed. There was no doubt in people's minds about the justness of their cause in World War Two. The cruel realities of life under German rule came as a shock to the Allies with their distrust of propaganda and to many Germans who had heard nothing but Nazi propaganda. Eisenhower was worried that people would not believe the truth about the camps and encouraged careful reporting. The *New York Times* gave an account of German reaction to Buchenwald.

'Some Germans were sceptical at first, as if this show had been staged for their benefit, but they were soon convinced. . . . Men turned white and women turned away. It was too much for them.

'These persons who had been fed on Nazi propaganda since 1933, were beginning to see the light. They were seeing with their own eyes what no quantity of American propaganda could convince them of. Here was what their own government had perpetrated.'

## Britons at War

Winston Churchill became prime minister of Britain on 10 May 1940. Chamberlain decided to resign because he was faced by a rebellion in his own Conservative party while the Labour party stated that they would only 'serve under a new prime minister.' Chamberlain had to advise the King on his successor. There were two candidates for office, Lord Halifax, the foreign secretary, and Winston Churchill. On 9 May 1940 Chamberlain asked Churchill whether he would serve under Halifax and Churchill, usually so ready to speak, said nothing as two minutes ticked by. Chamberlain then advised the King to ask Churchill to form a coalition government which George VI did the following day. Britain had her war leader and a small Cabinet of energetic men like the trade union leader Ernest Bevin, who became Minister of Labour and National Service, and the newspaper owner Lord Beaverbrook, who became Minister for Aircraft Production.

The government's powers in 1940 were considerable. Rationing, compulsory military service and control of imports were already in force. On 22 May 1940 an Emergency Powers Act gave the government virtually complete control over British citizens and their property. Churchill made himself Minister of Defence and took control of the military side of the war as well as the civilian side. He ran the British war effort in an amazing manner. He himself said: 'All I wanted was compliance with my wishes after reasonable discussion.' He expected people to argue out decisions with gusto and interested himself in everything from food rations to military equipment.

The British people responded to Churchill's energetic lead. He had the knack of putting into words what many felt and his slogans were quoted with pride. People accepted the blackout restrictions, the shortage of fuel, the food rationing, the clothing coupons and the utility standards for goods, because they were determined to win the war. The housing shortage and general

A poster warning civilians against casual talk about the war

bomb damage created serious problems but people made do cheerfully because they felt that it was their war. In 1941 clothes rationing was begun and a 'points' scheme was brought in for food not on strict ration. Everybody was given a number of points for a month and these could be used as people wished for the available food. In 1942 the Ministry of Fuel was set up to control coal production and by the end of the war men were conscripted into the mines. These men were called the 'Bevin Boys'.

In spite of controls and restrictions horse racing continued throughout the war and people struggled on packed trains so that they could take a holiday away from home. 'Music While You Work' became a popular radio programme in factories all over the country while Tommy Handley kept the nation laughing with the antics of Colonel Chinstrap, Mona Lot, Mrs Mopp and Funf on his programme, ITMA, 'It's That Man Again'. In June 1940 the Entertainments National Service Association, E.N.S.A., was formed to perform plays and variety shows to troops and factory audiences everywhere. An important move was made when C.E.M.A., Council for the Encouragement of Music and the Arts, was set up in 1939. Within a year, C.E.M.A. was giving 400 concerts a month to people in shelters, canteens and art galleries all over the country. Although paper was short there was a great demand for books and magazines which could be read while people sat in shelters, or waited on duty at fire-posts and in guard-rooms. Magazines such as *Horizon* and *New Writing* were very successful.

Morale was kept high by the fact that living standards for many people improved as the war went on. The evacuation of children from danger spots in the towns showed the public that slum conditions still existed in Britain while the air raids brought people together to fight a common enemy. The result

A poster encouraging mothers to leave their children safely in the country

Children being evacuated from the large cities

of this was that the government was encouraged to provide better conditions. Supplementary or extra pensions were introduced for old people and widows in 1940 and over one million people took advantage of this scheme. Cod liver oil, blackcurrant extracts and, later, concentrated orange juice from the United States were given out free of charge at food offices and welfare centres. From the middle of 1942 the health of the nation showed a steady improvement and wages increased at a greater rate than the cost of living. The war against Germany and her allies united the British people and brought about a general improvement in their standard of living.

In June 1941 the Government set up a Committee of Inquiry under Lord Beveridge to investigate problems of social security. Beveridge argued that the destruction of war had cleared the ground for an entirely new system. He proposed that there should be a single system of insurance covering all citizens. All those of working age would pay a single weekly contribution which would be recorded by a stamp on a card. In return benefits would be paid to the sick, the unemployed, and those who had retired. This plan gave people a real hope for a new world and gave British soldiers something to fight for. Churchill was wary of any ideas which appeared to be like the false hopes of 1918. He argued that the war must be won before any four-year plans were launched. In July 1945 the British people voted for a Labour government to carry out the promise of a better world set out in the Beveridge Report. World War Two had produced the blueprint for the Welfare State of today.

Women played a vital part in the war effort. At first they volunteered to join the Civil Defence and the Auxiliary Services, A.T.S., W.A.A.F., W.R.N.S., or worked in factories, hospitals and on the land. Later in the war, the compulsory registration of women was brought about by the government. Women could still volunteer for the services or be drafted by the Ministry of Labour to places that were short of workers. Women's work had become a vital part of the national war effort.

The spirit of cheerful comradeship and involvements brought about by the struggle and the danger is clearly shown in this account of the destruction of the Guard's Chapel by a flying bomb in 1944.

W.R.N.S., working on submarine maintenance

'Although I was still pinned down by debris, rescue work was progressing fast and it was with wonder that I gazed idly at a leg that had been uncovered and lay in front of me. It was dressed in a khaki silk stocking and shod with a brown brogue shoe. It looked lifeless. For a moment I thought of Pauline, but no, what would she be doing with khaki stockings? I looked again . . . That was my stocking, my shoe, my leg. And yet it was no part of me. I could not move it; I could not feel it. I tried to wriggle my toes. Nothing happened. Engulfed now with fear, I tried to convince myself that, yes, this was truly a nightmare, one from which I was bound soon to wake up. I think I must have been given a morphia injection for I still felt no pain, but I did begin to have an inkling that I was badly injured. I turned my freed head towards a Guardsman who was helping with the rescue work, and hysterically I cried out:

'"How do I look? Tell me how I look?"

'"Madam", he said, "you look wonderful to me!"'

## Out of the Line

Two groups of people were out of the widespread battle line of World War Two. Prisoners of war were forced to wait for the result of the war while spies had to work secretly for their side. The first group suffered from the restrictions of camp life. The Japanese starved and beat prisoners with little regard for humanity but the Germans and the Allies treated military prisoners fairly. A number of prisoners escaped in sensational ways like the group who dug their way out of a German camp under a wooden vaulting horse.

Franz von Werra was the only German prisoner who managed to escape home after being in a prison camp in Britain. He only managed to escape successfully when he had been taken to Canada early in 1941. From Canada he crossed into the U.S.A., which was still neutral, and from there made his way back to Germany. While in Britain von Werra managed to escape and get to an airfield where he bluffed his way into the cockpit of a Hurricane.

'Von Werra's heart thumped madly. His hands were clammy, his throat dry. Two more minutes! God grant nobody turned up.

'The mechanic manipulated the truck with conscious expertness, swinging it round the starboard wing in a graceful sweep, halting it dead, with a clatter of couplings, so that the trolley-acc. was in exactly the right position. He jumped off the truck platform, went behind to the trolley-acc. and raised the armoured cable over his shoulder, preparatory to plugging it in.

'The aircraft swayed. For a second von Werra did not grasp the significance of the movement. He opened the ignition pump a couple of times, hoping it would be enough. A voice above him on the port side said quietly:

' "Get out!"

'He jerked his head back. At eye-level on the left-hand side of the cockpit, the sun was reflected on a highly-polished button of an Air Force officer's greatcoat. It gleamed too on the muzzle of an automatic pistol.'

For most prisoners the war was a long period of waiting as this poem from a British magazine produced in Oflag VII B shows:

*Barbed Wire*, December 1944

Daylight again, and still the night goes on
A dream that knows no waking. Still we stare
Beyond the wire to the old world we knew

Long since when Life itself was fair,
And each new daybreak with the spreading light
Brought us the gift of one more day to spend—
To spend the way we would with song and friend
And well-loved hills to wander . . . God how bright
And clear the water ran in dales of Wye
Where primrose hides and dark trout haunts the stream,
And crazy walls go clambering to the sky,
Cloud envious as we. I dare not dream
Too much of that far world—God give me strength
To keep the one small flame of hope alight,
Defying this our dark, until at last
The one tomorrow comes and all is bright.

The second group of people out of the line were the spies. Both sides built efficient spy networks during the war and a cunning game of double bluff was played by men who worked unseen and often unrecognised. Great trouble was taken to feed the enemy with false information and as a result the truth was often unrecognised by both sides.

A poster warning soldiers against spies

# 12 Invasion of Europe

*' The war will be won or lost on the beaches.'*      Rommel, 1944

## Conference at Casablanca, 1943

For ten days in January 1943 the Anfa Hotel outside the Moroccan town of Casablanca hummed with activity. There were wonderful views over the sea and over the white buildings of the town set among green palms from the wide verandas of this hotel but few of the people there had time for the view. President Roosevelt and Winston Churchill discussed the conduct of the war with their chiefs of staff. The Germans and the Japanese fought their own wars with no real co-operation while the Allies carried out combined operations. In addition the American military leaders had decided as early as 1940 that if and when they entered the war they would concentrate on defeating Hitler and Mussolini before smashing Japan. Now at the Casablanca conference the British group, led by Churchill, argued that the Allies should attack Germany from the south by invading Italy in 1943. They also felt that the bombing of Germany should be continued and supplies sent to Russia until, in 1944, the difficult landings in France could be attempted. In the Far East it was suggested that the Japanese should be held and the Burma Road into China opened again. The Americans discussed these ideas thoroughly and by 24 January 1943 agreement was reached on all the main points and a landing in Sicily was planned for the spring. An American, Eisenhower, was placed in command of the Allied armed forces while an experienced British general, Alexander, was appointed his deputy.

The Germans had moved into Vichy France as the Allies conquered North Africa and the French scuttled their fleet at Toulon rather than let the Germans use it. In Morocco both de Gaulle and Giraud, another French general, claimed to speak for France. The conference ended with Churchill and Roosevelt arranging to sit in a smiling group with the two

furious French rivals before the press photographers. At the
final press conference Roosevelt unexpectedly outlined the
Allied aim as 'unconditional surrender'. The other leaders
quickly agreed to this aim so that there could be no misunder-
standing but the point had not been fully debated and it has
been claimed that the unconditional surrender demand encouraged the Germans to fight to the last.

## *The Russian Recovery*

While the Allies met at Casablanca beneath the Mediterranean sun the Russians fought grimly in the snows of Central
Europe. Stalin stated that he could not leave his country for any

— DER WASSERSCHEUE KLEINE WINSTON —

The German view of the second front. Stalin is pushing an unwilling Churchill into
action

conference and that all he wanted was the second front against
Germany. After the Russians had crushed the German Sixth
Army at Stalingrad Stalin increased his demands for an Allied
invasion of Europe to take the German attention off Russia.
He claimed that the British and Americans were reluctant to
fight and that they were content to let the Russians tear the
heart out of the German Army. The British and Americans
could answer that they knew how tough an invasion of Europe
would prove. Hitler's 'Atlantic Wall' was strong. In August
1942 a strong group of British and Canadian commandos struck
at Dieppe on the French coast. They held a small section of

the coast for a time but were driven back and the strength of the Germans in France had been proved. Stalin had to be content with supplies from his Allies. These came by the northern route to Archangel in spite of German submarines and warships based in Norway, by the long route across the Pacific and Siberia, and by the southern route from the Persian Gulf to the Caspian Sea along the Trans-Iranian railway. From June 1941 until April 1944, 6,430 planes were sent by the Americans for Russian use and Britain sent 5,800 more. Jeeps, lorries, tanks, steel, chemicals, food and clothing were all sent to help the Russians. With such supplies the Russian soldiers were able to meet the Germans on a more equal footing and to prove their fighting skill. They had used 'Molotov cocktails', empty vodka bottles filled with petrol and fused with a piece of cloth, against German tanks. Now they were able to use modern weapons and in the early months of 1943 the Russians regained 185,000 square miles of land from the Germans.

## German Counter-attack, July 1943

Hitler decided that this Russian recovery must be halted and that during the summer the Germans must regain their winter losses. He planned to trap the Russians where their advance bulged into the German line around Kursk. Tanks and guns were rushed from the factories straight to the front until the Germans had collected over two thousand tanks for their attack. The Russians poured supplies in to meet the attack and hundreds of thousands of railway wagons rolled from inside Russia into the Kursk salient carrying every kind of equipment. After German delays on account of Mussolini's wavering, the attack

Russian tanks move into action against the Germans

went in at the end of the first week in July 1943. There was bitter fighting and the citizens of Moscow rejoiced when they read the report of the first day's fighting:

'All the attacks were repelled with heavy losses to the enemy and only in some places did small German units succeed in penetrating slightly into our defence lines. Preliminary reports show that our troops . . . have crippled or destroyed 586 enemy tanks . . . 203 enemy planes have been shot down. The fighting is continuing.'

The legend that the Germans always advanced in the summer was destroyed and the Russians began their counter-attack. By October the Russians were in Kiev and some units pushed to within sixty-seven miles of the Polish border.

The Russian Front, 1943

After the Casablanca conference Stalin continued his demands for a second front. He refused to leave Russia to attend the Quebec conference in August 1943, and refused to attend the conference at Cairo in the same month to discuss the war with Japan, because Russia was not at war with Japan. At Cairo the Allied leaders met the Chinese leader, Chiang Kai-Shek, to discuss the war in the Far East. Foreign ministers met in Moscow in October 1943 and at long last in November the three Allied leaders met at Teheran, the capital of Iran. Churchill celebrated his sixty-ninth birthday at Teheran by holding a party at the British Embassy there. The Allies toasted each other many times and the joint statement issued after the conference ended: 'We came here with hope and determination. We leave here friends in fact, in spirit, and in purpose.' The Allies agreed to set up a 'family of Democratic Nations'. This agreement led to the first proposals for a new world organisation, which were drawn up at Dumbarton Oaks mansion in Washington in August 1944. Above all the Allied leaders were determined to defeat Germany and planned to renew their attack and prepare the second front in France which Stalin so badly wanted.

## Operation 'Husky', 1943

As agreed at Casablanca the American Seventh Army and the British Eighth Army were launched against Sicily in June 1943 fresh from their successes in North Africa. Montgomery and Patton, the American general who sported a pearl handled

Allied troops advance in Sicily.

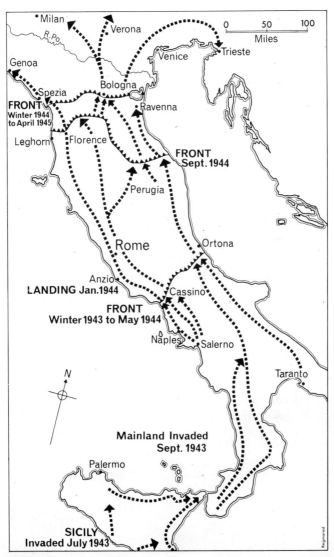

The Allied invasion of Italy

revolver in Western style, pushed on through Sicily. In spite of German delaying action these two able commanders drove the enemy out of Sicily in thirty-nine days. The Italians had no heart for the German war and on 25 July 1943 Mussolini was toppled from power by the Fascist Grand Council and King

Victor Emmanuel III. The Allies failed to take full advantage of this change of government and negotiations dragged on with the new Italian leader, Marshal Badoglio, while the Germans built up their strength in Italy. Finally the Italians agreed to terms and their fleet surrendered to the Allies. The Germans managed to sink the Italian battleship, *Roma*, north of Sardinia and the Italians found themselves fighting the Germans. Mussolini was rescued by a daring German commando raid and the Germans set up their own Italian Fascist government under a sad and tired Mussolini in the north of Italy. The long slog up the Italian mainland now began and the Allies found no easy way into the heart of Germany.

The mountainous country of Italy, with its steep valleys and rushing rivers, was ideal for defensive war and the Germans made the most of the situation. By the end of September 1943 the Allied armies held the southern part of the Italian mainland and on 1 October 1943 General Clark entered Naples. Grimly the Americans and the British struggled up Italy while their leaders planned landings in France. In an attempt to speed up the Italian advance the Allied forces made a leapfrog jump on 22 January 1944 and landed troops at Anzio behind

25-pounder guns move forward over an Italian river

The citizens of Rome welcome the Allied forces

the German defences called the 'Gustav Line'. The Germans managed to contain this landing and to hold the 'Gustav Line' centred on Monte Cassino. The monastery at Monte Cassino was bombed in February 1944 but the 'Gustav Line' was not broken until May, after weeks of savage fighting. In June 1944 the Allies were in Rome and British troops reached Florence in August, but by this date the main attack upon Germany in the west had been switched to France. The Italian campaign had proved a hard struggle but it had tied down fourteen good divisions of the German Army.

## Operation 'Overlord', 1944

During the early months of 1944 southern England became a vast military camp. Eisenhower claimed that 'a great human spring' was being coiled up ready for the attack upon Germany's 'northern wall', the French coast. Care was taken to keep the Germans guessing as to where the attack would strike. Near Dover a ghost army marched, built camps of cardboard, and sent radio messages on a special network. The Germans waited uneasily. They had sixty divisions in France and the Low Countries and were determined to halt the invading army on the beaches and the coastal fields which Rommel had ordered to be sown with more minefields and to be studded with giant stakes called 'Rommelspargel', Rommel Asparagus.

On the night of 1 June 1944 the B.B.C. news was followed by the usual personal messages in French for the underground. Amongst many meaningless sentences special messages were hidden and Canaris, the chief of German intelligence, had warned his men to listen to all these messages and to pick out lines from a poem by Verlaine, for this was the Allied warning of attack. On this night listeners all over France picked up the first line of Verlaine's poem and both the Germans and the French knew that the invasion would begin within forty-eight hours of the second line of this poem being broadcast.

The weather was stormy and the second line was not broadcast as everybody waited. Rommel decided to make a swift visit to see his wife on her birthday, 6 June. The weather was too stormy for an invasion. Near Portsmouth in his caravan Eisenhower studied the stormy skies and called for full weather reports. The situation was that there would be a slight clearance on 6 June and Eisenhower decided to go ahead with the invasion on that day. D-Day was to be Tuesday, 6 June 1944. The second line of the French poem, which had been written in the nineteenth century, was broadcast beginning with the words: 'Blessant mon cour . . .' (Wounding my heart . . .). The Germans refused to believe that the invasion could be taking place and Hitler was convinced that the Allies would only launch a raid in the style of the Dieppe raid.

Supplies and reinforcements for the troops in Normandy

On the way to France, June 1944

The great fleet of assault craft butted its way across the Channel. The Americans and British huddled in these craft suffered the agonies of seasickness before facing the withering fire on the Normandy beaches. On the eastern part of the Normandy invasion coast the British Second Army went ashore.

'There was a curious jubilance in the air. As the troops headed towards the beaches, the loudspeakers in a rescue launch off Sword roared out "Roll out the Barrel". From a rocket-firing barge off Gold came the strains of "We Don't Know Where We're Going". Canadians going to Juno heard the rasping note of a bugle blaring across the water. Some men were even singing. Marine Denis Lovel remembers that "the boys were standing up, singing all the usual Army and Navy songs". And Lord Lovat's 1st Special Service Brigade commandos, spruce and resplendent in their green berets (the commandos refused to wear tin helmets), were serenaded into battle by the eerie wailing of the bagpipes.'

Major King spoke words from *Henry V* into the loud-hailer on his landing craft heading towards Sword beach:

And gentlemen in England now a-bed
Shall think themselves accurs'd they were not here. . . .

The landings were made successfully in spite of the powerful German defence and supplies began to pour into the early

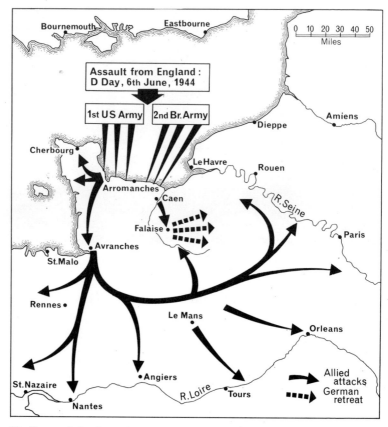

The Normandy landings

bridgeheads. 'Pluto' an oil pipeline, had been made to carry oil under the Channel. 'Gooseberry' harbours were constructed by sinking blockships while two huge concrete harbours were floated across the Channel. These 'Mulberry' harbours were vital to supply links until the Allies could clear a French port. One 'Mulberry' sank in the violent storms late in June but the other proved vital for landing supplies until Cherbourg was operating in August, 1944.

The Allied advance went forward. Eisenhower was able to use control of the air to destroy targets such as bridges in the rear of the German forces and so disrupt their defences. Yet the fighting was bitter. The British took Caen after a savage struggle and the Americans fought their way towards St Lo.

In this area the hedgerows and dirt banks made tank fighting impossible and every farm had to be taken by infantry assault. Still the advance went on and a German counter-attack was trapped by a neat pincer movement towards Falaise. The Americans and British closed the Falaise gap and two German field armies were taken.

On 15 August 1944 a further landing was made in the south of France near Toulon and soon the Allies were advancing up the Rhone valley to link with Patton's swiftly moving troops striking from the north. Four days after this landing the French in Paris took their part in the attack upon the Germans. The Free French Forces of the Interior went into action as Eisenhower's Sherman tanks rumbled towards Paris. On 26 August 1944 General de Gaulle was able to march through the streets of Paris amidst the deliriously happy population.

The Allied 'Blitzkrieg' swept on. Planes bombed objectives ahead of advancing tank squadrons and supplies were rushed to the front line by the Red Ball Express, a motorised column using 5,400 vehicles carrying fuel and ammunition. The Canadians took Dieppe in September 1944 and so avenged their defeated raid in 1942. The Allied commanders decided to turn the Siegfried Line, the fortified zone on the German frontier, by capturing the river crossings near Cleve. The American air-

Parachutes fill the sky as the Allies invade southern France

borne units were to take Eindhoven and Nijmegen while the British were to land further north at Arnhem. The landings at Eindhoven and Nijmegen were relieved by the arrival of advancing British tanks but a German counter-attack turned the ten miles to Arnhem into a slow slog. For nine days the Red Devils held out against German panzer forces, then those who were able to do so were forced to withdraw to the British lines. The Allied advance had overreached its supply lines and there was to be no quick sweep through to Berlin. In the autumn of 1944 the armies had to prepare for another winter's campaigns.

## The Russian Steam Roller

Throughout 1944 the Russians hammered the German eastern front. Early in the year they smashed the German defences near Leningrad then switched their push to the south and cleared

A Red Army unit drives Germans from a village

all south Russia by May. After this success they swung north again and beat the Finns soundly before pushing into Poland, Rumania and Bulgaria. The Hungarian people welcomed the

Russians and Yugoslav partisans under Tito fought their way through to join up with the advancing Russian Army. The Poles in Warsaw under General Bor rose in rebellion against the Germans as the Russians drew closer. The Russian Army then halted while the Germans wiped out the Polish forces in a terrible battle lasting sixty days. The Russians claimed that the Poles had risen against the Germans too soon but it is possible that they were not sorry to see a Polish force, which looked to London for support, destroyed. The Germans fought the Russians every inch of ground but by early February 1945 the Russians reached the Oder river in the north and were able to push south to link up with their allies advancing from the west.

# 13 Victory in Europe

Forty-five days after Allied soldiers had waded ashore on the Normandy beaches a group of German generals tried to kill Hitler. On 20 July 1944 a bomb in Count Stauffenberg's carefully placed briefcase exploded and Hitler's conference room was wrecked. The Fuehrer himself escaped with arm and ear injuries and the plotters were hounded down. Hitler was very shaken and was ordered to rest. While in bed Hitler turned his attention to the situation on the front in France. The German army was still in good order. Allied probes at Arnhem under Montgomery and at Metz under Patton had been blocked and the Germans still had more divisions in defence than the forty-eight Allied divisions which were pushing on into Germany. Hitler decided to set a counter-attack in motion during the winter of 1944 and chose the area of his early 'Blitzkrieg' success of 1940 as the place for the attack.

## The Battle of the Bulge

The Americans practised rifle shooting in the front line on what they termed their 'phoney front'. Fog and snow made conditions in the Ardennes unpleasant as 16 December 1944 dawned. The Germans had planned to infiltrate the American lines in this area and Skorzeny, the S.S. officer who had been in Mussolini's rescue party, trained a party to carry out this operation. Later American counter-security led to a number of incidents and Montgomery had to acquire a special identification card in order to move about the front.

Then in the Ardennes area;

'A mailed fist struck in the early hours of December 16, 1944, a blow which sent the world reeling.

'Roaring cannons along an eighty-mile front served as the alarm clock for thousands of sleeping American troops that murky morning. It electrified men who felt safe in the assurance that theirs was a rest area. Commanders and their staffs tumbled out of bed to eye with wonder the flashes of the distant artillery and listen, amazed, to reports from their outposts. They didn't wait long; shortly after six o'clock the first reports were hastily relayed back to the command posts that through the early morning dark could be seen the German infantry, moving forward slowly. Behind them snorted the tanks, ready to roar through the gaps cleared by the infantry. In at least one instance, the infantry were driving a herd of cattle before them to detonate any mines which might have been planted in the earth by defending troops.'

The surprise German counter-attack was a success and the Allies fell back in confusion. In places they felled trees as anti-tank barriers in desperate attempts to stem the German advance. The defence in the area of St Vith checked the Germans and the Americans grimly held on to Bastogne as the Allies began to recover from the surprise of this German attack. The commander at Bastogne was called upon to surrender by the Germans. He replied with the one word, 'Nuts!' Then the Allies struck back at the flanks of Von Runstedt's army and by January 1945 the German thrust in the Ardennes area had been defeated. Hitler had to move divisions to the east to halt a new Russian attack and so abandoned any plans of destroying the American and British invasion forces.

The Allied leaders at Yalta. Churchill, President Roosevelt, Marshal Stalin seated

# *Yalta Conference, February 1945*

The ring was closing in on Nazi Germany and the Allied leaders met at Yalta in the Crimea to discuss the settlement of Europe. Stalin, Roosevelt and Churchill met together in a cheerful mood although differences between the Allies were beginning to appear. However, the Allied leaders agreed that a further conference should be called to meet at San Francisco in April 1945 to discuss a charter for a world organization based upon the ideas set out at the discussions at Dumbarton Oaks at an earlier date. They also agreed that Germany should be split into three zones for Allied occupation under a Central Control

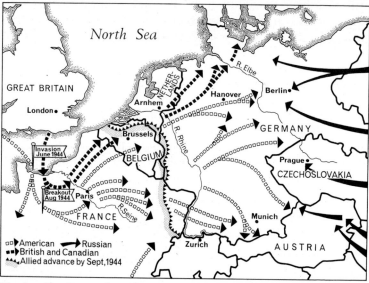

The ring closes in upon Germany

Commission. France was to be offered a fourth zone if she wanted it. Russia agreed to join the war against Japan in return for certain territories in the East. The eastern frontier of Poland was to be drawn along the Curzon Line of 1919, while liberated countries of Europe were to be helped to set up democratic governments based on free elections.

At this time the Yalta meeting was regarded as the peak of the Allied war effort. The conference was considered a success and only later did critics question this and term the Yalta meeting 'Stalin's greatest victory'. It can be argued that the agreements at Yalta gave Stalin the chance to arrange for the Russian domination of eastern Europe but it can also be argued that the Russian armies were in eastern Europe anyway. Furthermore, at the time of Yalta, Germany had still to be defeated.

## The Final Moves

A final attempt to break German morale was made by Bomber Command. On 14 February 1945 Dresden was devastated and

Bren gunner in action against the Germans, February 1945

over 100,000 people were killed. The Germans fought on. In the west the British and Americans reached the Rhine in February 1945. The Germans regarded this great river as their main line of defence and they blew up the bridges and prepared to hold the line to the last.

On 7 March 1945 Sergeant Drabik led his platoon of American infantrymen through enemy fire to the banks of the Rhine at Remagen near Coblenz. He had been ordered to take up defensive positions but found to his surprise that the Germans had not finished the demolition of the bridge over the Rhine at Remagen. Promptly the sergeant led his men across the bridge and so took a Rhine crossing. He told the story afterwards in flat unemotional terms: 'We ran down the middle of the bridge, shouting as we went. I didn't stop because I knew that if we kept moving they couldn't hit me. My men were in squad column and not one of them was hit. We took cover in some bomb craters. Then we just sat and waited for the others to come. That's the way it was.'

Within twenty-four hours 8,000 men were across the Rhine and Eisenhower could say that 'the traditional defensive barrier to the heart of Germany had been pierced'. The bridge itself only lasted ten days under a merciless pounding from German planes, rockets and guns. However, it made a bridgehead possible and American engineers soon built bridges in support. The British and Canadian divisions under Mont-

General Eisenhower chats with General Montgomery

gomery swung through Holland and struck north towards Denmark and Lubeck. They crossed the Rhine on 23 March 1945.

Meanwhile the Russian armies rolled westwards into Germany. On 25 April 1945 Russian and American patrols met and shook hands at Torgau on the Elbe, seventy-five miles south of Berlin. Thirteen days before this President Roosevelt had died from a stroke and in honour of his leadership the American press placed his name at the head of their daily list of war casualties. Roosevelt's Vice-President, Harry Truman, took on the great load of office as the war drew to its close in Europe.

Mussolini was shot by Italian partisans on 28 April 1945 and two days later Hitler shot himself as the Russian armies closed in on Berlin and reduced the city to ruins. Admiral Doenitz

Marshal Zhukov signs the German unconditional surrender terms on behalf of the Russian government

took over command of the German forces and began the search for terms. He hoped to split the Allies by making peace with the British and Americans before coming to terms with the Russians. The Allies stood firmly together and early in the morning of 7 May 1945 the Germans officially surrendered to Eisenhower at his headquarters in a Rheims school. All along the front the German commanders surrendered. On 4 May 1945 the German forces on the British front surrendered to Field-Marshal Montgomery. On 8 May the German military leaders signed the surrender terms in Berlin under the watchful gaze of Marshal Zhukov. Though the Allied leaders had planned to announce victory together the news of the surrender at Rheims leaked out and the western world rejoiced on VE-day, Victory in Europe day, 8 May 1945. The Russians celebrated a day later. The war in Europe was at an end and the Allies turned their full attention to Japan.

# 14 Victory in the Pacific and the Peace

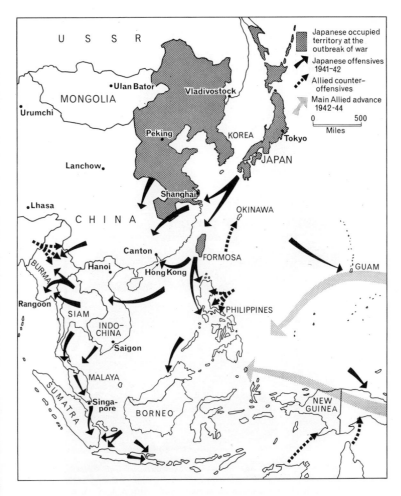

Counter-attack in the Pacific

Once the Japanese advance had been checked the task in the Pacific was to work out a satisfactory means of counter-attack. These counter-attacks had to be amphibious and General MacArthur worked out a plan of advance in a series of leapfrog hops. Japanese island strongholds were to be bypassed and their supply lines cut. American forces in the Pacific were carefully built up for this attack and by August 1944 there were nearly 100 American carriers operating in the Pacific.

The Allied advance began in 1943 and pushed steadily forward. The Japanese fought savagely and resorted to suicide charges, 'Banzai' charges. Tarawa in the Gilbert Islands was a small group of Pacific islets joined by a coral reef round a lagoon. The Japanese fortified the central island with concrete

An Australian infantryman shakes hands with a U.S. Army paratrooper

forts roofed with iron rails laid on coconut logs. The Americans bombarded these positions on Tarawa and then sent marines ashore on 21 November 1943. The Japanese had survived the bombardment and the landing troops met a withering fire. They had to take the Japanese positions one by one using flame throwers and long iron pipes containing explosive called Bangalore torpedoes. Nearly 1,000 Americans died in the assault upon Tarawa and over 2,000 were wounded. The lessons learnt from this assault helped the planning of future attacks and naval engineers, the Seabees, prepared the island as a base for the advance. By early 1944 the Americans and Australians had reached the Marshall Islands and the Carolines. On 21 October 1944 General MacArthur landed in the Philippines and early in 1945 Manila was taken.

The British had fallen back from Burma to India. This front was low down on the list of priorities for supplies but in March 1943 Brigadier Wingate began a guerrilla war behind the Japanese lines. His long range groups, called Chindits after the Burmese word for lion, struck at Japanese communications and were supplied from the air. After a year of this successful campaign Wingate was killed in a plane crash in Burma. The British Fourteenth Army fought on through 1944 under General Slim and drove the Japanese back from Imphal. Early in 1945 Burma was cleared of Japanese troops.

Supplies were still sent to the Chinese over the mountains by air and along the Ledo Road built by the American, Stilwell. The Chinese war effort against the Japanese was far from satisfactory in spite of these supplies, for their interests were split. The Nationalist government under Chiang Kai-shek attacked the Chinese communists who were especially strong in the north-west. This split made a Japanese thrust possible in the spring of 1944. The Japanese struck hard and managed to cut across China and to gain control of the coast from Korea to Malaya. In spite of this Chiang Kai-shek insisted on using his troops against the Chinese communists and asked that his American chief of staff, Stilwell, be recalled. Fortunately these problems in China did not halt the main advance against Japan and the Japanese were not strong enough to make full use of their success in China.

At dawn on 19 February 1945 the Americans launched an

attack upon Iwo Jima, an island of volcanic ash only 750 miles from Tokyo. The Allies were knocking on the inner ring of the Japanese lines of island defences. Iwo Jima was a Japanese fortress and the U.S. Marines had to fight for every inch of it. The moment at which the American flag was raised on the topmost ridge of the extinct volcano on the island was caught by a press photographer in a picture that has since become famous.

A group of U.S. marines plant the Stars and Stripes on the topmost ridge of Iwo Jima

Over 4,000 Americans were killed before Iwo Jima was cleared and the next island objective, Okinawa, cost the lives of a further 12,000 men.

Preparations were being made for the Allied attack upon Japan itself when President Truman decided to use the weapon which British and American scientists had developed under the Manhattan Project. The President felt that the use of such a weapon would save further loss of life on the scale of the losses at Okinawa. On 6 August 1945 the first atomic bomb was

U.S. marines in action against the Japanese

dropped on the Japanese city of Hiroshima. Three days later a second bomb was dropped on Nagasaki. The only two atomic bombs in existence at the time brought the war to an end. The age of atomic weapons began as World War Two finished.

Just over three years after the attack on Pearl Harbour the Japanese surrendered formally to General MacArthur on the battleship *Missouri* anchored in Tokyo Bay. MacArthur pre-

A flamethrower is used against a Japanese strongpoint

General MacArthur signing the Japanese surrender terms on board the *Missouri*, 2 September 1945

sided over the ceremony flanked by the American commander of Bataan and the British commander of Singapore. These generals had just been released from Japanese prison camps and they each received one of the five pens MacArthur used to sign the surrender terms. Sunday, 2 September 1945, was termed VJ Day to mark the formal surrender of Japan. World War Two was over and a changed world began to emerge from the ruins of the conflict.

## Making the Peace

Millions of people had died in World War Two. One out of every twenty-two Russians, one out of every 150 Britons and one out of every 500 Americans had been killed before Germany and Japan were defeated. During this struggle the Germans had lost one out of every twenty-five of their people and the Japanese one out of every forty-six. Cities and communications in many parts of the world were in ruins and many people were homeless and stateless. The war had brought fearful human suffering and at its close many found themselves forced to linger in 'displaced persons' camps or even to remain in prisons under new rulers. The Nazi menace had been defeated at great cost and many of the victors found little joy in the postwar world.

The Allied leaders met at Potsdam, a suburb of Berlin, in

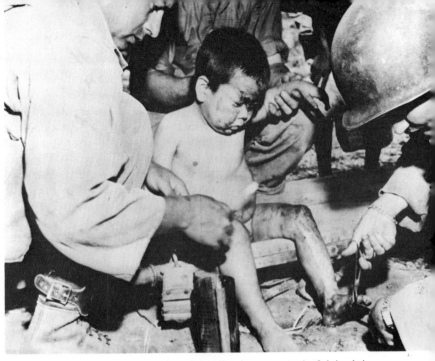

The suffering brought by the war was fearful. A child wounded in the fighting being treated by the Americans

July 1945 to discuss the peace settlement. Stalin represented Russia and President Truman represented the U.S.A. Britain's

Winston Churchill and a section of the crowd celebrating victory, 1945

war leader, Churchill, was defeated in the parliamentary election held in July 1945. His party, the Conservatives, were soundly defeated at the polls by a people who were determined to see social reform without delay. His place at Potsdam was taken by the new prime minister Attlee. Of the Allied war leaders only Stalin remained to build the peace. At Potsdam the decisions taken at Yalta concerning Germany were confirmed and the zones of occupation outlined. Berlin was in the Russian zone but was divided into sectors which were to be administered by the Allied powers. No agreement was reached over the matter of the Polish frontier with Germany but the Poles were allowed to administer the lands up to the line of the rivers Oder and Neisse. A council of foreign ministers was set up to discuss peace treaties with Italy, Bulgaria, Finland, Hungary and Rumania. The U.S.A., Russia, Britain, France and China were represented on this council. Discussions dragged on and the five treaties were not finally signed until early in 1947. The settlement with Germany, Austria and Japan was complicated by the growing division between the Allies.

In 1946 Churchill made a speech at Fulton in the United States in which he spoke of an 'iron curtain' which had fallen across Europe. World War Two was not followed by a swift and tidy peace settlement and the growing diplomatic hostility between Russia and the western powers gained the name of the Cold War. This hostility made a final settlement in Europe virtually impossible, though in 1955 a treaty was signed with Austria. Under the treaty the Austrians had to pay heavy reparations to the Russians. The Allies made their own terms with their areas of occupation in Germany in 1949. In May, France, Britain and the U.S.A. set up the German Federal Republic in Western Germany, while in October the German Democratic Republic was formed in the Russian zone. The divided city of Berlin was a symbol of the split between East and West and already in the period 1948–49 the Russians had tried to cut off supplies to Berlin from the West. The western powers had mounted a massive air lift which kept Berlin supplied but this great effort was sad proof that world peace had not arrived with the ending of World War Two.

The Americans were virtually in sole control in Japan and this meant that they were able to arrange the settlement there.

In 1947 a new democratic constitution was introduced in Japan and the Japanese economy was rebuilt with American aid. In 1951 a peace treaty with Japan was signed. Forty-nine nations signed this treaty though the Russians refused to do so. Again the clash between Russia and the western powers was shown in the Far East by the Korean War, 1950–53. The Russians had agreed to join in the attack upon Japan at the end of World War Two. Their troops occupied North Korea where a communist government was set up. In 1948 Russian troops withdrew, leaving Korea divided between the communist north and the south under the rule of the American-backed Syngman Rhee. In June 1950 the North and South Koreans were at war and Russia and Communist China gave support to the North while the U.S.A. and other members of the United Nations tried to gain a cease-fire by giving support to the South Koreans. In the Far East an uneasy peace followed the victory in 1945.

## Vengeance

As the war ended in 1945 people began to take revenge for their suffering under Nazi rule. There was an official hunt for a number of German leaders who were to be tried as war criminals. At Nuremberg, between November 1945 and October 1946, twenty-two German leaders were put on trial. Only twenty-one, headed by Goering, were present as Borman, the Deputy Führer, could not be traced and so was tried in his absence. The Nuremberg trials and the other trials of war criminals in Germany brought out the full horror of Hitler's rule. Separate trials were also held in Japan. At these trials in Japan and Germany a number of war leaders were condemned to death. Eleven were sentenced to death at Nuremburg and of these Goering managed to escape the gallows by taking poison. These trials annoyed some people who felt that enemy war leaders should be shot without full trial while others felt that such trials were of doubtful legality and that war crimes only should be punished. The spirit of vengeance gradually burnt low and the sad figure of Hess, still in Spandau Prison in Berlin, remains to remind people of the Nuremberg trials. Hess was Hitler's original deputy and taught himself to fly a Messerschmitt fighter so that he could fly to Scotland in 1941 in a vain attempt to arrange peace.

# A Changed World

Why cannot the one good
Benevolent feasible
Final dove descend?

And the wheat be divided?
And the soldiers sent home?
And the barriers torn down?
And the enemies forgiven?
And there be no retribution?

Because the conqueror
Is an instrument of power,
With merciless heart hammered
Out of former fear,
When to-day's vanquished
Destroyed his noble father
Filling his cradle with anguish.

From *The War God*: STEPHEN SPENDER

So far the story of the peace makes sad reading. Yet the Cold War and the widespread seeking of revenge are only one aspect of this period. There is a more hopeful aspect. The spirit of co-operation produced by the war years did not die completely. The Charter of the United Nations Organization was signed by fifty nations in June 1945. The member states declared that this new organization was 'determined to save succeeding generations from the scourge of war, which twice in our lifetime has brought untold sorrow to mankind.'

The Cold War has been carried into the debates of the United Nations but a great deal has been done through the special agencies of the U.N., like U.N.E.S.C.O. (United Nations Educational, Scientific and Cultural Organization) and W.H.O. (World Health Organization) to help nations all over the world. Such agencies carried on the work started by the 'biggest piece of first aid in history' which was done by the United Nations Relief and Rehabilitation Administration and the International Refugee Organization in the two years after the war. These two agencies saved Europe from starvation and saved millions of lives. The divisions of war still remain today and at the same time some of the co-operation brought by war remains. Perhaps the co-operation among men will strengthen in the face of the complete destruction of modern war.

THE WRECKED WORLD

**AND NOW TO WORK** (Copyright in All Countries)

# Further Reading

There are an enormous number of books on World War Two and many of them have been made into films. You might make a list of the World War Two stories that you have read and the films you have seen about the War. Do they help you to understand the years 1939–1945?

The following list of books may help you to start to find out more about the war. Remember that older members of your family and their friends may be able to tell you stories about their part in World War Two.

*General*

WINSTON CHURCHILL: *The Second World War.* 6 vols. Cassell, 1948–54.
C. FALLS: *The Second World War*, Methuen, 1950.
D. FLOWER AND J. REEVES: *The War 1939–45.* Cassell, 1960.
W. LANGSAM: *Historic Documents of World War II.* Van Nostrand, Anvil Books, 1958.
K. SAVAGE: *The Story of the Second World War.* O.U.P., 1957.
D. SCOTT-DANIELL: *World War II.* Benn, 1966.
L. L. SNYDER: *The War: A Concise History 1939–1945.* Robert Hale, 1962.

*Special Interests*

M. CARVER: *El Alamein.* Batsford, 1962.
B. COLLIER: *The Battle of Britain.* Batsford, 1962.
C. HIBBERT: *The Battle of Arnhem.* Batsford, 1962.
R. JUNGK: *Children of the Ashes.* Penguin (Pelican), 1963.
W. LORD: *Day of Infamy.* Henry Holt, 1957.
D. MACINTYRE: *The Battle of the Atlantic.* Batsford, 1961.
R. MERRIAM: *Battle of the Bulge.* Panther, 1959.
A. MOOREHEAD: *The Desert War.* Hamish Hamilton, 1965.
FIELD MARSHAL VISCOUNT MONTGOMERY: *Memoirs.* Collins, 1958; Fontana Books, 1960.
W. PRULLER: *Diary of a German Soldier.* Faber, 1963.
C. RYAN: *The Longest Day.* Four Square Books, 1962.
A. J. P. TAYLOR: *The Origins of the Second World War.* Penguin, 1964.
A. WERTH: *Russia at War.* Pan Books, 1965.
C. WILMOT: *The Struggle for Europe.* Collins, 1952; Fontana Books, 1959.

138

*Film*

Rank Film Library. *The Second World War:* Part I, *Prelude to Conflict* (25 mins.); Part II, *Triumph of the Axis* (21 mins.); Part III, *Allied Victory* (22 mins.).

*Filmstrips and Recordings*

Commonground. 'Second World War'. C & B 918.

B.B.C. Radio for Schools, Autumn Term 1967, 'Contemporary History'.

A film produced by the Commonwealth War Graves Commission is available for hire by schools and other non-paying audiences. The film, mostly in colour, traces against a background of war cemeteries and memorials the history of some of the operations in which Commonwealth forces died during the two world wars. Further particulars and information on the work of the Commission is available from: Commonwealth War Graves Commission, 2 Marlow Road, Maidenhead, Berks SL6 7DX.

# Index

# Index

# World War Two: Time Chart

| YEAR | WAR IN WESTERN EUROPE | WAR IN EASTERN EUROPE | WAR IN MEDITERRANEAN AREA |
|---|---|---|---|
| 1939 | SEPT: British troops land in France | SEPT: Germany attacks Poland<br>NOV: Russia attacks Finland | |
| 1940 | APL: German invasion of Norway and Denmark<br>MAY: German invasion of Western Europe<br>JUNE: Dunkirk evacuation | MAR: Russo-Finnish Peace Treaty<br>AUG: Russians annex Baltic States | JUNE: Italians invade France<br>NOV: Italians invade Greece<br>DEC: British offensive opens in North Africa |
| 1941 | JULY: U.S. forces relieve British in Iceland<br>DEC: Germany and Italy declare war on U.S.A. | JUNE: Germany attacks Russia<br>SEPT: Leningrad besieged<br>DEC: Russian counter-attack at Moscow | JAN: British take Tobruk<br>FEB: Germans land in North Africa<br>APL: Germans invade Yugoslavia and Greece<br>MAY: Germans capture Crete |
| 1942 | AUG: Dieppe raid<br>NOV: Germans occupy Vichy France | JULY: Germans capture Sevastopol<br>SEPT: Germans attack Stalingrad<br>NOV: Russian counter-attack at Stalingrad | JUNE: Germans take Tobruk<br>OCT: Battle of El Alamein<br>NOV: Allied landings in French North Africa |
| 1943 | JAN: Casablanca Conference<br>DEC: Teheran Conference | JAN: Russians relieve Leningrad<br>FEB: Germans surrender at Stalingrad<br>JULY: Russian victory at Kursk | JAN: British enter Tripoli<br>MAY: Axis forces in North Africa surrender<br>SEPT: Allied invasion of Italy<br>Italian surrender |
| 1944 | JUNE: D-Day landings<br>JULY: Caen taken<br>DEC: German offensive in Ardennes | JAN: Leningrad completely freed by Russians<br>JULY: Russians enter Poland<br>OCT: End of Warsaw rising | MAR: Cassino destroyed<br>JUNE: Allies enter Rome<br>AUG: Allies invade S. France |
| 1945 | FEB: Yalta Conference<br>MAR: Allies cross Rhine<br>APL: Russians and Americans meet at Torgau<br>JULY: Potsdam Conference | JAN: Russians take Warsaw | |

MAY 8 GERMAN ARMED FORCES IN EUROPE SURRENDER

| WAR IN PACIFIC AREA | WAR AT SEA | WAR IN THE AIR |
|---|---|---|
|  | OCT: *Royal Oak* sunk<br>DEC: *Graf Spee* scuttled |  |
| JUNE: Japanese occupy bases in Indo-China | FEB: *Altmark* incident<br>JULY: Royal Navy attack French Fleet at Oran<br>SEPT: British receive 50 U.S. destroyers<br>NOV: Battle of Taranto | MAY: Bombing of Rotterdam<br>AUG: ⎫<br>  ⎬ Battle of Britain<br>SEPT: ⎭<br>DEC: Bombing of Coventry |
| DEC: Japanese attack British, Dutch and U.S.<br>Attack on Pearl Harbour<br>Fall of Guam and Wake Island<br>Fall of Hong Kong | MAR: Battle of Matapan<br>MAY: *Bismarck* sunk<br>DEC: *Prince of Wales* and *Repulse* sunk | MAR: R.A.F. raids on Ruhr |
| JAN: Japanese invade Burma<br>FEB: Fall of Singapore<br>APL: Fall of Bataan<br>MAY: Battle of Coral Sea<br>JUNE: Midway Island Battle<br>AUG: U.S. landings on Solomons | FEB: Java Sea naval battle<br>NOV: French fleet scuttled at Toulon | MAY: First 1,000-bomber raid on Cologne |
| MAR: Battle of Bismarck Sea<br>JULY: Allied forces attack in New Guinea | SEPT: Italian fleet surrenders<br>DEC: *Scharnhorst* sunk | MAY: R.A.F. destroy Eder Moehne dams |
| FEB: Americans invade Marshall Islands<br>JUNE: Japanese retreat in Burma<br>AUG: Guam recovered | NOV: *Tirpitz* sunk | JUNE: 'V1' bombardment begins<br>SEPT: 'V2' bombardment begins<br>British airborne attack on Arnhem |
| JAN: Burma Road reopened<br>MAR: Conquest of Iwo Jima<br>JUNE: Conquest of Okinawa |  | FEB: Dresden destroyed<br>AUG: Atomic bombs dropped on Hiroshima and Nagasaki |

SEPT 2 FINAL JAPANESE SURRENDER